DY|NG

**FINDING
LIFE'S MEANING
THROUGH DEATH**

|TO

L|VE

ANDY
CHALEFF

Meaningful
Relations

ENDORSEMENTS

"*Dying to Live* is a book every living being should read to find freedom from the fear of death. With a message both simple and profound, Andy Chaleff offers a path toward liberation from the anxiety we all inevitably face. After reading it, I feel more at ease with death than I ever did before."

- SATISH KUMAR,
FOUNDER OF SCHUMACHER COLLEGE AND
LIFELONG PEACE PILGRIM

"This book is extraordinary, it's a treat, and it affects me deeply. Reading it, I feel I am going on a journey with a wise, caring, and perceptive friend whose honest opening of his own struggles with the deepest questions of life and death have not failed to stir the same reflections in me about my own. I warmly recommend you all go on this journey with Andy and within yourself soon, as carefully and enjoyably as I have. Wonderful, gracious, gently helps you to free yourself, bit by bit!"

- ROBERT THURMAN,
AUTHOR OF *INNER REVOLUTION* AND *MAN OF PEACE*

"Reading *Dying to Live* felt like sitting with a close friend who isn't afraid to talk about the things we usually avoid. Andy Chaleff doesn't just write about death—he invites us into an intimate conversation with it, and somehow, with ourselves. Brave, beautifully written, and profoundly illuminating."

- AUSTIN HEARST,
MEDIA EXECUTIVE AND PHILANTHROPIST

"The words draw you in with a morbid fascination—just as they must have done for Chaleff while he was writing them. You plunge forward like a moth to the flame. But in the end, what awaits is a beautiful peace. As I turned the final page and closed my eyes, two lines from a Tagore poem drifted in: "My grief becomes my blessing today, in Impenetrable Death, I smell the Elixir of Life." Go on Andy, take us there."

- SUGATA MITRA,
TED PRIZE-WINNING EDUCATIONAL INNOVATOR

"Our modern world treats death like a glitch in the system. But Andy Chaleff reminds us that death is the great clarifier—the one truth that can reorder our priorities and reconnect us to what matters. This book is an invitation to stop performing life and start inhabiting it."

- CHIP CONLEY,
FOUNDER OF THE MODERN ELDER ACADEMY (MEA)
AND AUTHOR OF LEARNING TO LOVE MIDLIFE

Dying to Live: Finding Life's Meaning Through Death
by Andy Chaleff

ISBN: 979-8-9885720-0-8 Paperback
ISBN: 979-8-9885720-4-6 Hardback
ISBN: 979-8-9885720-5-3 Ebook

Published by

Meaningful
Relations

www.meaningfulrelations.com

CONTENTS

INTRODUCTION

When I shared my desire to write this book with friends, I saw faces instantly transform from smiles to frowns. Death is not a subject people are—forgive the pun—dying to talk about. Yet, as with all my previous books, there was something within me that insisted this be written. Throughout my life, death has hovered somewhere between fear and curiosity for me. I have been both intrigued by this enigma and frightened by what I might discover when looking at it. I know I'm not alone in this.

I must confess, this book holds few answers to life's most pressing questions, such as what happens after death or the ultimate purpose of life. Instead, it explores some of the thoughts I believe many of us secretly want to voice: recurring thoughts too difficult to voice in casual conversations. My aim is to provide insight into the ways we process death—how we cope with grief, find meaning in loss, and integrate the inevitability of death into our daily lives and our understanding of the world around us.

My life has been touched by significant loss, starting when I was quite young. Both my parents have passed away, along with many others who were dear to me. This certainly doesn't make me an expert on death. But it has given me profound—albeit unwanted—experience. In every book I write, I strive to offer an unguarded glimpse into my psyche— revealing my fears, shame, and confusion. I find it more meaningful to share my deepest vulnerabilities than to teach or preach. My greatest hope is that by exposing what lies behind the curtain of my ego and allowing myself to be vulnerable, you will gain a deeper understanding of yourself. Perhaps you'll recognize thoughts you've had but never fully explored or discussed with others.

I believe in the universal human experience that connects us. Though we may come from different walks of life, we share fundamentally similar experiences. These experiences uncover the universal humanity we all share: the hidden pain, fear, and doubt beneath society's acceptable facade.

Reflecting on my life, I've come to realize that death lies at the heart of my deepest emotions. With every layer I peel back, there it is, at the very core. This book emerges from that realization—offering us a chance to spend a few hours together exploring a topic often pushed aside.

In reading this book, you'll discover the basics—like how embracing the reality of death can lead to a richer, more meaningful life. But beyond that, I hope you see how death is the leverage point for so much more. It is the spark that ignites everything beautiful in life, even the pain. Especially the pain.

I spent several years writing this book because I realized it was more than just a book. It was a state of being. In these chapters, I present a way of being that I hope will bring you closer to what you might call your higher self, your deeper sense of knowing. Each chapter is written as a meditation, short and juicy. My intention is for you to take the absence of text as an invitation to fill it with your innate awareness.

My greatest intention with this book is for you to move beyond the words on the page, into your internal realm. Sit with the questions you may have pondered in passing but never had someone to explore them with. I am now with you in that exploration.

I believe your life will be richer for having read this book and spending this time together. By reflecting on death, we welcome the urgency of life. We are compelled to shed the parts of ourselves that weigh us down. The parts that must die so that we can truly live, harking back to the title of this book: *Dying to Live*.

The book is designed to allow for non-linear reading, so feel free to jump to chapters that catch your eye. But it also traces my personal journey with death: my initial fear, gradual acceptance, and eventual embrace of it as a guide.

At the end of each chapter, you will find a section dedicated to reflection. I firmly believe that questions are one of the greatest gifts we can offer one another, as they provide a unique opportunity to connect with ourselves and gain clarity. To facilitate this connection, I have included a selection of questions for you to choose from. While each question offers valuable insights, I encourage you to focus on the one that resonates most deeply with you. Take this opportunity to meditate on it or write down your thoughts in the space provided. This practice will help you delve deeper into your reflections and ground your experiences throughout the book.

As we embark on this journey together, I hope our time spent in these pages proves as enriching for you as writing them has been for me. By revealing so much of myself, I invite you to know me—and, I hope, to better understand yourself.

Let us begin.

CHAPTER 1

My First Loss

I WAS SIX years old when I first encountered death. It was an ordinary day. I had just finished school when my mother and grandmother came to pick me up. As I climbed into the back seat of the station wagon, the air felt heavier than usual—laden with an unspoken sadness. Their grave expressions immediately caught my attention.

My mother's trembling voice broke the silence: "Apricot died today. She was hit by a car."

Apricot was our beloved family dog. Overwhelmed by this sudden loss, I burst into tears, the emotions flooding through me too intense to comprehend. This is one of my earliest childhood memories.

This was also when I first experienced a peculiar mental state I call the "gray zone." It's a sense of blankness that seems to originate from the front of my head, most intensely felt behind my right eye. Like a haze, this gray fog clouds everything. It emerges in moments when life's events are too sudden and uncontrollable to make sense of immediately. It's a noisy mix of confusion, fear, loneliness, and helplessness. In this case, it was triggered by the agonizing thought: *I will never see Apricot again.*

The gray zone revisits me whenever I face sudden loss. Even

though I know the feeling, it always catches me off guard. Instantly, I feel out of body, as if my entire being is protesting the loss. This was my first introduction to a feeling that would visit me many times afterward.

Once my initial tears subsided, my mother and grandmother were incredibly supportive. To distract me, they took me to Sears to go shopping.

"Can I get a toy?" I asked, looking up at my mother with hopeful eyes.

"Of course, sweetheart," she replied, smiling gently. "You can pick whatever you like."

I wandered through the aisles, finally settling on the game Operation. I held the box in my small hands, feeling a strange mix of emotions.

"Are you sure you want this one?" my mother asked, noticing my hesitation.

"Yes," I said, nodding slowly. "But… it feels weird."

"Weird? How so?" she inquired, kneeling down to my level.

"I feel happy about the new toy," I admitted, "but I'm also still sad about everything."

My mother hugged me tightly. "It's okay to feel both happy and sad at the same time. Buying this toy is just a way to bring a little joy back into your life, not a reward for your grief."

I looked up at her, trying to understand. "So it's okay to be happy about it?"

"Yes, it's okay," she reassured me. "It's important to find moments of happiness, even when we're sad."

This early experience was my first real confrontation with the complexity of emotions, a lesson that took most of my life to truly grasp. Even today, the ability of emotions to coexist—happiness and sadness, relief and regret—can catch me off guard. It was not until much later that I learned the importance of witnessing these emotions without judgment, allowing them space without trying to figure them all out.

Years later, during a heartfelt talk with a friend whose mother had died after a long bout with cancer, this lesson came back to me.

"You must be relieved," I suggested, noting the end of her mother's suffering.

She replied with a weary sigh, "It feels wrong to feel that way, but yes, I am. I've been wishing for her peace, and now, I feel guilty for those wishes. I would give anything for just one more day with her."

From the loss of Apricot to the present day, I've experienced many losses—too many to list in this book. With each loss, I found myself back in the gray zone of my childhood, where numbness once protected me from pain. Over time, I've come to experience grief as a companion, a reminder of how deeply I loved that person.

But this grief isn't always accessible. Sometimes, the pain is so immense that my system won't allow it in all at once. It's like the moment that you contract your muscles before the impact of a car crash and then spend the following months recovering from the strain.

The next step, demanding a deeper level of self-compassion, involves transforming this confusion and pain into gratitude. Gratitude fundamentally shifts the energy these emotions carry. I use the word "carry" because this pain often feels like a heavy burden within me. A friend recently shared his experience with the persistent thoughts following his breakup, saying, "She's living inside my head, and she isn't even paying rent." This is how I would describe unresolved pain within me.

Shifting from the world of pain and confusion to gratitude has been my way of turning the world upside down and having it make even more sense. It allows emotions to move through my system and helps me find meaning in the suffering. By embracing gratitude, I acknowledge the love and joy that were once present, transforming my pain into a reminder of the deep connections I've had. This shift doesn't erase the loss but integrates it into a broader understanding of my life's journey.

Shifting my grief to gratitude has not been a straightforward process. As I write this, I feel a sense of anxiety, thinking of readers who have recently lost someone and can't yet imagine this shift. For me, it has been about understanding and accepting life's paradoxes. Each loss taught me to blend sorrow into a deeper part of my character, increasing my compassion and my ability to hold space for others' suffering. It allowed me to feel more deeply into moments of happiness—friends' laughter, peaceful mornings, the joyful chaos of family—making them even more special because of life's impermanence.

This transformation was neither easy nor swift. It was a gradual recognition that joy and pain are not opponents but partners in the dance of life, shaping our emotional experiences and making us more deeply human. By embracing this transformative process, I discovered a path to peace, enabling me to live fully with loss while keeping my heart open to all that life offers, both joyful and sorrowful.

The loss of Apricot marked the beginning of a crucial life theme for me: coming to terms with death. Over the next fifty years, I had to learn how to metabolize the pain of loss. The first step in that journey was giving the emotions space to be. I think of these painful emotions as a scared child hiding under the covers. Instead of acting like a frustrated parent and pulling them out of bed, I see myself sitting in the corner, waiting for the child to get up when they feel safe.

I've learned that emotions, like the seasons, cycle through our lives—each with its own hue and temperament. They descend upon us like autumn leaves, each color representing a different feeling: crimson anger, golden joy, somber gray. To witness them without judgment is the beginning of a journey toward finding peace. Embracing this natural rhythm teaches us the beauty of impermanence and offers a glimpse of gratitude for all those we have lost.

MEDITATIVE QUESTIONS

Reflecting on Early Loss

Think about your first encounter with loss. How did it shape your understanding of grief and mortality? What emotions do you remember feeling during that time?

The Gray Zone

Have you ever experienced a state similar to the "gray zone" described in this chapter, where emotions and thoughts become overwhelming? How do you usually cope with such moments?

Complexity of Emotions

Reflect on a time when you felt conflicting emotions simultaneously, such as happiness and sadness. How did you navigate these mixed feelings, and what did you learn from that experience?

CHAPTER 2

What Happens When I Die?

AT THE AGE of 13, one night around 3:00 a.m., I was abruptly pulled from a lucid dream into sheer panic. I sat up in bed, hyperventilating, my heart pounding so fiercely I could hear it, each beat resonating through my body. This was a fear and anxiety deeper that I had ever imagined possible. Lying there in the dark, the thought that had yanked me from sleep echoed in my mind: *What happens when I die?* The idea suffocated me, filling me with such intense anxiety that each breath felt as if it could be my last. Over and over, the thought spun in my head: *I will not exist for eternity.*

I was desperate to sidestep this thought. My mind raced for alternatives. *Maybe there's a god, a heaven. Maybe my soul will continue after death.* Yet, deep inside, I frantically tried to reassure myself, grasping for hope that seemed implausible. My questions grew more logical and probing. *What's more likely—that the universe emerged from a Big Bang, or that a magical being wished us into existence?* I found myself leaning toward the cosmic accident version of events, a thought that chilled me to the bone: If this life is all I have, then I'm doomed to an eternity of nothingness.

Facing this emptiness felt like looking down into a dark hole—only to realize the ground beneath me was crumbling, leaving me more scared than before. These night terrors would creep in during the early hours, a constant reminder of the emptiness that haunted me.

One night, many years later, I shared these fears with my brother during a rare moment of vulnerability. His response was simple and detached from my emotional state: "You don't need to worry about it. You won't even realize it because you'll be dead."

"That's exactly what terrifies me," I admitted, my voice barely a whisper. "The thought of just… not existing. And eventually, even the memory of me will be gone eventually."

That conversation was a turning point in my journey with death. I realized that by avoiding my fear and not facing it directly, I had allowed it to grow into a monstrous shadow, eclipsing any hope for peace. My fear of non-existence had grown too big to contain, flooding my mind with fear.

Recently, a friend shared that his son was battling similar fears. "My son has a deep fear of death," he confessed during one of our calls. "He was having terrors one night, and I found him hyperventilating in his room. He didn't want to talk about it at first."

"How did you handle it?" I asked, curious and empathetic.

"It wasn't easy," he replied. "I didn't want to pressure him, but I could see it weighing on him. Since I didn't know what to say, I've given him time to move through his emotions. It feels quite helpless."

Although my experience mirrored his, I couldn't find the words to offer advice. When I revisit that moment in my life, the feelings rush back, raw and intense. I needed space. I needed to move through this in my own time and at my own pace. It wasn't a problem that could be solved with a wise saying or quick fix. It was like grappling with an invisible weight. It required patience and understanding. The only thing I knew to do was to simply be there for him, offering unwavering support and love.

This brings me to a core theme in my life, one that we'll revisit throughout this book: my self-love practice. This practice revolves around embracing the things I resist most. I explore this concept in detail in my previous books, particularly in *The Wounded Healer*. The idea is that confronting our innermost fears serves as a catalyst for healing. By acknowledging and accepting uncomfortable truths and fears, we can achieve a more integrated self. This notion of an integrated self can be challenging to grasp, so let's put it this way: it's about becoming a person who is comfortable in their own skin.

In my daily life, this process takes the form of an unsettling thought or fear that surfaces in my consciousness, such as, *I am a terrible writer*. If I attempt to dismiss or reject this thought, it seldom vanishes. Instead, it retreats into the shadowy corners of my mind, lurking in the spaces I seldom visit consciously. Practically speaking, this might lead me to spend excessive time reading through the drafts of a book or possibly even not sending it out for fear of being exposed. In this way, the thought festers and gathers strength. When I think about these sabotaging thoughts, I imagine an army quietly assessing the defenses of a fortress. These hidden fears probe for vulnerabilities in my psychological defenses, seeking an opening to break through and confront me.

This was especially true with my fear of death. This phenomenon manifests most powerfully when I am at my most vulnerable—during sleep. In the quiet of the night, when the guards of rational thought and busy distractions are down, these fears mount their assault. They emerge not as coherent thoughts but as visceral sensations that inevitably jolt me awake in a state of panic.

This pattern highlighted an essential truth: by attempting to seal off these fears, I inadvertently strengthen them. They grow in the dark, fed by the very isolation meant to contain them. Recognizing this, I began to shift my approach from one of avoidance to one of engagement. I learned to sit with my fears, to invite them into the light of my conscious awareness. In the case of my writing, I have accepted that by saying "I am a terrible writer, and that's okay." I do not say this to make it true but rather to calm the voices in my head. We will get more into this practice later in this book.

Facing what frightens me head-on has required both courage and self-compassion. By welcoming these fears into my consciousness, I start a conversation between my current self and the parts of me still trapped by old anxieties.

Embracing these shadow parts with compassion has taught me that self-love isn't just about feeling comfortable and safe, it's about building resilience and staying calm in the face of life's inevitable challenges. It's about realizing that every fear has something to tell us, showing us our deepest wants and worries.

Through this practice, I've learned not only to manage my fear of death but also to appreciate life more deeply. Just as a storm eventually gives way to calm skies, we must let our fears emerge and dissipate. By facing and accepting these fears, we enrich our lives, adding a depth that comes from truly understanding our impermanence.

"I'm scared of death, and that's okay."

MEDITATIVE QUESTIONS

Exploring Fear of Death

Reflect on your own fears about death. When do these fears tend to surface, and how do they affect you physically and emotionally?

Confronting the Unknown

How do you typically react to thoughts about the unknown or unknowable aspects of life and death? What strategies can you use to face these thoughts more openly?

Dialogue with Fears

How can you start a compassionate dialogue with your fears, inviting them into the light of your awareness? What steps can you take to face and understand these fears more deeply?

The Day Everything Changed

THERE ARE MOMENTS in life that completely redefine us—events so intense they change our future. One such moment for me was April 8, 1989, a date etched in my memory because it altered the course of my life forever: it was the day I learned that my mother had been killed by a drunk driver.

If I were to draw a line tracing how I became the person I am today, it would all stem from that single, shattering moment. Had it not happened, I likely would not have left the US at age 20, nor would I have pursued a path of deep introspection, and this book would never have been written. My life felt like the board game Life. Everything had been tossed into the air, leaving me to reinvent my next moves.

As we get older, we often begin to view our life in reverse, creating a story from the fragments of our experiences. It's like assembling a puzzle to form a coherent narrative. These moments often make sense in hindsight, giving our story—and consequently, our lives—meaning. But in the moment, it can feel unbearable.

Reflecting on this period of my life and the lessons it imparted,

I am reminded of the classic parable of "The Farmer and the Horse." There once was a farmer who had a horse. One day, the horse ran away, and his neighbors came to offer their sympathy.

"What bad luck!" they said.

The farmer replied, "Maybe. We'll see."

A few days later, the horse returned, bringing with it several wild horses. The neighbors came to celebrate with the farmer.

"What good luck!" they said.

The farmer replied, "Maybe. We'll see."

The next week, the farmer's son was trying to tame one of the wild horses, but he was thrown off and broke his arm. The neighbors came to offer their sympathy.

"What bad luck!" they said.

The farmer replied, "Maybe. We'll see."

A few days later, soldiers came to the village to conscript young men into the army. Because of his broken arm, the farmer's son was not taken. The neighbors came to congratulate the farmer.

"What good luck!" they said.

The farmer replied, "Maybe. We'll see."

The story highlights the idea that events themselves are neither inherently good nor bad, and their ultimate impact can't be judged immediately. This perspective encourages patience, acceptance, and openness to the unfolding of life's events.

At the time, I was too young to grasp the full significance of this loss in my life. Even now, it remains a challenge. Yet, this event marked a pivotal shift in my life journey, leading me to explore various spiritual paths and philosophies. Each book, each sermon, each meditation offered a lens through which I could view my grief not as a burden, but as a gateway to deeper understanding. I discovered that while the pain might never fully disappear, it could evolve into something less overwhelming and more meaningful.

The more I learned, the more I realized that my relationship with death was not just about my mother's passing. It had turned into a deeper exploration of my own approach to life and mortality.

With this came a sense of urgency to live with intention and to cherish the transient nature of existence. Experiencing death up close stripped away the trivial concerns that once seemed significant, sharpening my focus on what truly mattered—love, connection, and authenticity.

Throughout this journey, I began to see the fable of "The Farmer and the Horse" more clearly in my own life. I started to release the grip of my old narratives, the ones that told me my mother's death was the end of my life. It took some time, but I began to see that it was the beginning of a new life that I had yet to fully understand. This shift was not immediate, nor was it easy. It was a process of releasing, layer by layer, the heavy cloak of grief that I had wrapped myself in.

As I allowed myself to heal, I began to forge a new relationship with my memories of my mother. I focused on the joy she brought into my life, the lessons she taught me, and the strength she exemplified. These memories, once painful to recall, slowly transformed into sources of inspiration and motivation. I realized that my mother's spirit could continue to live on through my actions and the choices I made. This book being an example of just that.

Now I am at a point in my life where I am grateful for what all this has brought me. And if you were to ask me if this is the end to this story, I would say, "Maybe. We'll see."

MEDITATIVE QUESTIONS

Defining Moments

Reflect on a moment in your life that completely redefined you. How did it change your path, and what new directions did it lead you to explore?

The Farmer and the Horse

How can the parable of "The Farmer and the Horse" apply to your own life experiences? Can you think of an event that seemed negative at first but later revealed a positive aspect, or vice versa?

Finding Meaning in Loss:

In what ways have you found meaning in the losses you've experienced? How have these losses shaped your perspective on life and mortality?

CHAPTER 4

Our Evolving Relationship with Death

EVERYONE READING THIS book will be coming to it at a different stage in their lives. The way we perceive and interact with death varies widely depending on our age, personal experiences, and cultural background. Your experience with this book and your understanding of death will likely be influenced by your life's journey, your religious beliefs, your health, and your experiences with losing loved ones. Our relationship with death is not static but evolves continually throughout our lives. Even mine has evolved since I began writing this book.

Although there are no clear stages like the ones one might find when grieving loss, there are some phases which I have seen in my own life. I have broken these down into six phases, not knowing if there would come a seventh if I were to live long enough.

Early Encounters:
The Shadow in Storytelling

My earliest recollection of death did not come through a personal loss but through the poignant and traumatic scenes depicted in children's movies. One of my first and most jarring encounters was through the film "Bambi." The death of Bambi's mother was not just a plot point; it was a sudden, unanticipated jolt that introduced me to the concept of mortality. As a child, I felt this loss deeply, empathizing with Bambi and unconsciously projecting his loss onto my own family. It was the first moment I realized that my mother could disappear. This experience laid the foundational stone of what death meant—an abrupt departure, an irreversible loss.

I now also see that, at that age, I was longing for this truth not to be so. There was a desire to look to magical thinking as a means of reversing this reality. I remember feeling that if I concentrated deeply enough, I would be able to breathe life back into Apricot. I also remember the blanket that I carried with me as a child became the symbol of Apricot for me, and I never left it anywhere. I still have that same blanket today.

One of the most memorable and chilling experiences of my adolescence revolved around a Ouija board. At a neighbor's sleepover, curiosity and peer pressure led us to ask the board morbid questions about death. My heart pounded as I considered asking about my own death. The fear of having an answer, of possibly knowing the unknowable, was both thrilling and terrifying.

With a mix of dread and excitement, I finally asked, "When will I die?" My eyes locked onto the board, fixated on the first number the dial might move towards. Would it be 2, 3, 4? The thought of knowing how many years I had left sent shivers down my spine. As the dial began to move, my courage faltered, and I quickly took my hands off and left the room, my mind racing.

The anxiety of knowing haunted me, the idea of counting down to a specific year for the rest of my life was unbearable. At that moment, I truly felt the profound fear of the unknown.

Early Teenage Years: The Unspoken Truth

Growing up, no one talked about death. Adults avoided the topic, and there was no guide on how to handle the emotions it brought up. This silence made me uneasy and filled me with a sense of dread. Death became a scary and mysterious thing that adults whispered about but never explained. This taught me to fear death and see it as something best left unexplored.

As a teenager, my encounters with death took on a new dimension. The religious teachings from Catholic church on Sundays provided a framework of afterlife and moral consequence, yet they clashed with my burgeoning sense of skepticism. I've always felt a sense of unease when anyone asked me to believe something that I could not experience firsthand. I still feel that way today.

Simultaneously, my morbid curiosity led me down darker paths. I stumbled upon the infamous "Faces of Death" video series, where death was not hinted at but shown in its most raw and unfiltered form. I consumed these tapes in secret, like hidden stashes of adult magazines, a guilty exploration of life's final moments. In this morbid curiosity, I was flirting with a very scary part of my emotions. I was playing with fire, feeling the heat and thrill, knowing I could get burned.

As most people who know me will attest to, I have never been one for superficial conversation. This was true for me from a young age. Between the ages of fifteen and eighteen, I often pondered the vastness of the universe, leading to a sense of existential overwhelm. Questions like "Where is the end of the universe?" and "What lies beyond that?" filled me with deep anxiety. These thoughts were not shared with others, partly due to concerns about how they might react. It was a lonely time, filled with profound helplessness as I stared into the abyss of nothingness alone. This introspective struggle characterized much of my early years and I have rarely shared it with others because it has always been a sensitive part of my being.

Later Teenage Years: The Search and the Major Life Event

The trauma of contemplating an eternity of nothingness was something I chose to confront during my first year at university. I say "eternity of nothingness" instead of death because those words hit hardest. I enrolled in a Sociology of Death course, which felt like preparing to jump out of an airplane. It was a scary decision, but I was determined to make peace with this anxiety in my life. Ironically, it was during this course that I lost my mother to the drunk driver.

This period was followed by an incredible journey of pain mingled with self-discovery. My girlfriend at the time bought me ten books on grief recovery and finding meaning. I went through each one, from *On Death and Dying* by Elisabeth Kübler-Ross to *The Grief Recovery Handbook* by John W. James and Russell Friedman. Though the books made logical sense, I couldn't find the space to make peace with their messages of acceptance and surrender. Titles like *When Bad Things Happen to Good People* by Harold S. Kushner, *A Grief Observed* by C.S. Lewis, and *Man's Search for Meaning* by Viktor Frankl resonated with me, yet the concepts felt distant, like nice words that were too far away from my present reality.

This experience is a concern for me as I write this book. I recognize that some readers might be in the same place I was then, finding the messages challenging to grasp and apply.

At some point, trying to make sense of this loss began to feel senseless, so I ran away. At 20 years old, I left America and never returned to live there. I abandoned the pain of the past and started with a clean slate, deciding that if I only have this one life to live, I might as well see what I can experience before I die.

Building My Identity: Denial and Avoidance

Not long after my college graduation, I shifted from spending time contemplating death to focusing on building myself into something—though I wasn't entirely sure what. Of course, I was driven by the need to prove my father wrong about his assessment of my "wasted life," but there was more to it. This phase of my life was marked by a lot of blindness. I was accumulating experiences and successes, but in reality, I was running away from my past. I was constructing my self-worth through achievements, missing the point that no amount of success could fill the void I left behind when I exited the US.

I harbored a hidden belief that if I ran hard enough and fast enough, I could outrun the past. This period was driven by an incessant desire to make death irrelevant. I often see this same reaction in others when discussing the subject of this book. There's usually a hint of dismissiveness or a speck of judgment about why this topic would be valuable to anyone. I recognize this because it mirrors where I was when I was busy proving myself. Who has time to contemplate death? Why would you want to?

Even today, I am reminded of this daily. My last book, *The Connection Playbook*, has won several book competitions and is poised to sell many copies. Yet, as my wife walks out the door this morning, she says to me, "Why don't you write about something more appealing like the last one? Death is such a downer."

Her comment is a stark reminder that the journey of understanding and accepting death is not a popular one, but it's essential. It's a path that many avoid, yet there is invariably a moment when that is no longer possible.

Transitioning Out:
Understanding the Inevitability

"So now what?"

Those are the words often heard when we end our formal working careers, when the job that once gave us our sense of identity comes to an end. This happened to me at an early age—35 years old. Yes, I was young and incredibly active afterward, but I was no longer working for anyone, doing things I didn't enjoy, or making decisions based on money. That has now become my definition of retirement.

In the months and years after leaving my last real job, I was confronted with a new reality. People who once picked up my calls instantly were now too busy to speak. Those who would drop everything to listen to me were now nodding graciously and checking their watches. I faced the grim truth that many valued me not for who I was but for the value my position brought to their lives. Now that the position was gone, my importance in their lives had diminished.

It is a big moment. How do we reconcile this loss and find the energy to begin the next phase of life with the backdrop of pain from the prior one? The questions can run deep: *Is it that easy to replace me? Was I ever really needed? Was that worth giving so many years of my life?*

I have come to see this as an intermediary phase, or in religious terms, purgatory—somewhere between two places, not quite in either. It's like when a person leaves a long-term romantic relationship and is still processing the last partner, unable to fully dedicate themselves to the next. This phase is unique because it is full of loss, which is very challenging to process. There are dimensions to it that make it difficult. We will touch on mourning this type of loss throughout this book. The process of letting go of a past self and surrendering to an uncertain future is not easy. In fact, many people, confronted with this, die soon after retirement. But I have found that there is something special waiting for those who are able to make it to the other side.

Last Moments:
Embracing the Inevitable

My wife always says, "I can't wait to turn 50 years old. I read that at 50, people's happiness increases." I smile when I hear this, thinking it's less about age and more about people's circumstances: the kids are grown, there's less to prove, and more flexibility, if money has been saved.

And, at least in my case, retirement was more about having quality time. Time to finally make space for myself. Time to reconcile the pain that I left when I first ran away from the US. The ten years following the departure from my last job were lived like a monk. Though I never wore a white robe, I spent time with my thoughts, not being driven by them but marinating in them.

It was in this slowing down that I began to find joy again. This joy had a strong connection to my childhood, a feeling I had forgotten for most of my adult life. It had become so distant that I could no longer access it in my body.

With this newfound spaciousness, new inspirations began to emerge. I am now driven to write, speak, and educate others about the challenges one might need to overcome to find peace. One of those challenges is captured in this book, my homage to death. Many people, like myself, navigate their lives through inspiration, writing books, and discussing their past. Others find hobbies and sail gently into the sunset. When the demands of society are no longer pressing, people can find motivation from within. By making more space for this kind of motivation, I have learned to live with greater intention and authenticity.

This brings me back to where we began in this chapter. Our relationship with death is not static; it evolves continuously throughout our lives. It is deeply intertwined with our personal stories, cultural backgrounds, and different stages of life. While my journey started with fear, it didn't end there. Your path may look different from mine. What's important to understand is that our perception of death is shaped by our individual identities and life experiences. I cannot definitively conclude this discussion, as my life continues to unfold.

I have outlined six phases of my relationship with death throughout my life, and I anticipate a seventh might emerge if I find myself on my deathbed. Unfortunately, I likely won't be able to write about that phase, so we'll have to leave it to the imagination of each reader.

MEDITATIVE QUESTIONS

Current Phase and Impact

What phase of your relationship with death do you believe you are currently in? How does this phase influence your perspective as you read this book?

Personal Phases

Reflect on the different phases of your relationship with death. How has your perception of death evolved, and what events have influenced these changes?

Early Encounters with Death

What was your first experience with death, either personal or through media? How did it shape your initial understanding of mortality?

CHAPTER 5

Next in Line

IF YOU LIVE long enough, a secret invitation will eventually find its way to your door. Think of it as an exclusive club, to which you would prefer not have membership. I call this silent secret "being next in line."

It happens slowly. At first, a few friends my age died—some through accidents, others due to illness. Two of my close friends from high school passed away the year after we graduated. For years afterward, I thought, *That just as well could have been me.* Over time, while they were never completely forgotten, they became less connected to my current life, evolving into romanticized memories.

As more and more people begin to die around you, it gets closer and closer to reality, and you realize, *At some point it's going to be my turn.* It's reminiscent of the Agatha Christie novel *And Then There Were None*, but instead of eight characters, it's everyone in your life, and you are one of the main characters.

It was through these growing losses that I began to grasp my own fragility and found myself questioning, *How much time do I have left? When am I going to pick the short straw?*

The first to go were my grandparents. Throughout my twenties, I braced for the passing of their generation. When they did pass, I frequently heard remarks like, "They lived a full life," or "They were suffering, so it's also a blessing." Beneath each comment was the implicit acknowledgment that it was their turn to go.

Since my mom had already died, thoughts about my father soon began to surface. How long will I have him? As time passed, several of my friends' parents also passed away, bringing the reality closer to home. Having at least one parent alive gave me a sense of security. Even if my relationship with my father was rocky, there was comfort in knowing that, in the worst-case scenario, he was still there.

Then the day came when he too passed away from a heart attack at age 73. Afterward, I felt profoundly alone. Whatever illusion I had that I was still a child was gone. Then it hit me—I was now the next in line. There were no more buffers. Adding to this realization was the unsettling awareness that younger generations now saw me as next in line.

Losing both my parents was incredibly painful for many reasons: I lost my sense of security, the end of our shared traditions, and the deep-seated desire for the unconditional love that only parents can give—the kind that reassures you everything will be okay. With both of them gone, that external source of reassurance vanished, and I had to find it within myself. No matter my achievements, I always felt somewhat childlike while my parents were alive. Their passing marked a loss of innocence and forced me into an adulthood I had long resisted.

Adjusting to being next in line has been challenging. It's also partly why I wrote this book: How do I embrace being next in line? How do I step into the adulthood I so longed to delay?

I see this transition as shifting from creating an identity for myself, as I did in my 20s and 30s, to deconstructing it. Think of it like building a house brick by brick during my younger years— each achievement, title, and role adding to the structure. Now, it's about carefully dismantling that house to reveal the foundation underneath.

This process of deconstruction involves letting go of everything

I once thought was important. It's quite paradoxical. I built myself up to feel that I had a sense of meaning and purpose, only to reach the summit and realize, *Oh, now I must let go of all that to make peace with my inevitable death.*

Saying goodbye to the identities I have created throughout my life has been a process. As mentioned in the previous chapter, retirement is often the moment that ignites this journey of letting go.

My neighbor Phillip told me for years how excited he was to retire. He said, "I can't wait until I'm no longer tied to endless meetings, tight deadlines, and the constant stream of emails."

A few weeks after his retirement, I noticed Phillip on the street and I asked, "Hey, are you enjoying retirement?"

He sighed. "I thought I'd be ecstatic when I retired, finally free to do whatever I wanted."

"Isn't that the dream?" I said. ""No more early mornings or stressful meetings?"

"That's what I thought. But now that it's here, I feel... lost."

"Lost? How so?" I asked, my brow furrowing.

Phillip leaned forward. "The things I used to complain about—my job, my responsibilities—they were actually a big part of who I am. Without them, I'm not sure who I am anymore."

I've noticed that this transition is easier for those who are less attached to their status and work identity. The million-dollar question is, *How do I make peace with this transition?*

I cannot speak for others, but I can share some of the things I've observed myself doing. As my wife Rani and I have moved houses, I've come across items I've collected throughout my life—awards from my track and field days, certificates of achievement, mementos from earlier times. Initially, opening these boxes filled me with melancholy and a longing to cling to those special times in whatever way I could.

But after revisiting these boxes year after year, I realized the personal mementos they contained no longer represented who I am. It struck me that everything in that box would be discarded when

I died. A part of my identity stored away in a closet, something to reminisce about, a story to tell.

Then, in a deep moment of surrender, I knew it was time to let the boxes go. It wasn't easy. Rani resisted, perhaps seeing these items as a way to remain connected to me after my death.

"Why are you throwing these away?" she asked, her voice tinged with sadness.

"I feel it's time," I replied. "These things don't define me anymore. I am ready to let them go."

"But they are a part of your history," she insisted, tears welling up in her eyes. "They remind me of everything you've accomplished."

I took her hand and said, "It's time to let this go. It's not about erasing the past but making space for the present and the future."

Reluctantly, she agreed, and we orchestrated what I could best describe as a funeral service for the box. We sat together, sharing memories, laughing and crying, as we let go of the physical reminders of a chapter of my life. It was a mix of sadness and beauty, a symbolic gesture of moving forward. Letting go of this part of my past didn't mean it never happened or wasn't appreciated. It simply meant that I no longer needed to see myself in that way.

This feeling of letting go has always been bittersweet. The best way I can describe it is feeling at peace with not being. If I had to express this sentiment through music, it would be the song by the rock group Kansas, which tells us, "All we are is dust in the wind."

For many, this realization can be deeply unsettling—even terrifying. For me, it's like coming home. I lost myself only to find myself back again.

I've noticed that each farewell becomes increasingly challenging, the greatest being the eventual loss of my beloved wife. Yet, saying goodbye to her has also brought us closer. In bidding her farewell to here changing identities, I've allowed her room to grow and evolve. I've learned to let go of who she is today to make room for who she might become tomorrow. I won't pretend this is easy. Far from it. But I can say that it keeps me present and constantly grateful.

This brings us back to being the next in line. This realization can either empower or cripple us. It's a fork in the road. If we do not choose, it does not mean the road will not be chosen for us. And remember, if you have not already received the invitation, it will one day land on your doorstep.

MEDITATIVE QUESTIONS

Being Next in Line

Reflect on the concept of being "next in line." How does acknowledging your mortality impact your sense of purpose and daily actions? How does it influence your relationships with others?

Deconstructing Identity

Consider the idea of deconstructing the identity you have built over the years. What elements of your life do you feel ready to let go of, and how might this create space for new experiences and growth?

Letting Go of the Past

Reflect on any physical or emotional mementos you hold on to from your past. How do these items or memories define you, and what would it mean to let them go? How might this process help you embrace the present and future?

CHAPTER 6

The Luxury of Reflecting on Death

WHEN ASKED, AND I am often, "Why reflect on death?" My answer is invariably, "Because I have that luxury." Reflecting on death is not something everyone has the opportunity to sit with. For those caught in the relentless pursuit of survival, pausing to contemplate mortality can seem not just impractical, but a bit absurd. Typically, this privilege arises with a certain level of financial and environmental stability—at least, that has been my experience. However, this is not true for all. Viktor Frankl's remind us that profound reflections on life and death can occur even in the worst of conditions.

Viktor Frankl, a psychiatrist who survived the Holocaust, was stripped of all semblances of stability and security. Yet, it was under these extreme conditions that he developed his influential theory on the human search for meaning. In his famous work, *Man's Search for Meaning*, Frankl proposed that even in the depths of a concentration camp, people could find a fundamental purpose and a personal sense of meaning through their attitude towards suffering. He famously stated, "When we are no longer able to change a situation, we are challenged to change ourselves."

As I have gotten older, I have noticed that many of the personal discoveries I thought I had made on my own were actually made centuries earlier. It makes sense. If it makes sense now, why wouldn't it have made sense back then. Stoicism is a great example of this. The wisdom of the ancient Greeks gives us a powerful blueprint for navigating the ever-looming presence of death.

At its heart, Stoicism champions the cultivation of inner resilience through the mastery of one's emotions. It teaches that while the whirlwinds of fate toss us unpredictably, our true power lies in controlling our internal seas—our reactions and attitudes. This is reminiscent of Frankl's observations while in the prison camps.

The Stoics view mortality not as a grim specter to be feared but as a natural, essential aspect of life's rhythm. Death, in the Stoic view, underscores the urgency of living a virtuous life. It is a reminder that every moment is precious, every action meaningful. Thus, Stoicism does not diminish life's value by acknowledging death; rather, it enriches our living moments through this recognition.

In practical terms, Stoicism focuses on four key virtues: wisdom, courage, justice, and temperance. These virtues help guide a Stoic's daily life and shape their view of death. Wisdom helps us understand and navigate life's challenges; courage gives us the strength to face death without fear; justice ensures we treat others fairly and with empathy; and temperance teaches us to enjoy life's pleasures in moderation, always aware of our eventual end.

I got to experience this firsthand in a mountain village in Spain, where time seems to unfold at a gentler pace. I met an elderly potter named Ana. In her workshop, she shared her philosophy, reminiscent of the Stoics. "Each pot I craft,' she said, "is born from the earth and will one day return to it, just like us. We are here to shape our lives as best as we can, knowing they are as fleeting as the morning mist over the mountains."

I live with deep gratitude that I am here and able to reflect on what society might consider trivial matters. Death, in its inevitability, has spurred some of the most profound actions of my life, serving as a stark educator about the impermanence of life.

At the age of 52, my friend and mentor, Cees de Bruin, was diagnosed with Non-Hodgkin's lymphoma and given a prognosis of five years to live. Those around him maintained a hopeful demeanor, urging him to embrace the "long time" he still had. I didn't buy it.

I felt the pain of his impending loss as if it were already a reality, refusing to cushion the blow with a deferred timeline. Right then and there, I made a choice. I told him, "We are going on a trip."

"A trip?" he asked, looking puzzled.

"Yes, a trip," I confirmed. "We've spent the last decade working together and never taken a trip together. Just you and me."

He looked a bit confused at first, then with a broad smile, he said, "Let's do it."

I chose not to dwell on the timeline given by his doctors. Instead, inspired by a surge of clarity, I acted. We traversed the US national parks and expansive landscapes, places where the enormity of nature invited peace and reflection on life's transient beauty.

As we stood together on a mountain peak, surrounded by breathtaking vistas, Cees turned to me with a look of profound gratitude. "I never thought I'd see this," he said, his voice choked with emotion. "Thank you."

One evening, while we were sitting by a river, he opened up to me in a way he never had before. "You know," he began, "I've never told you how much you mean to me. I have never told you how much I feel cared for by you."

On that journey, I captured my favorite photo of Cees: seated cross-legged on the edge of a cliff, overlooking a vast canyon. His contemplative silence spoke volumes, perhaps pondering the same eternal cycle Ana had described, where all things begin and end with the earth.

Merely days after our return, Cees passed away unexpectedly from a heart attack. By the doctor's estimations, he still had four and a half more years to live. The opportunity to contemplate life without him before his departure, and to act on it, was a profound gift from death itself. Had I not allowed the sadness to guide me, I might have suppressed my feelings, opting for hope over the acceptance of reality. Instead, I followed a deeper intuition, understanding more than my rational mind could grasp at the time.

Of course, this sense of urgency was not unfamiliar to me. It had been instilled in me from a young age. While in the Sociology of Death class in college, I was confronted with the reality that I would eventually lose everything dear to me—most painfully, my mother. It was in that raw moment, without pausing for over-analysis, that I composed what would unknowingly be the last letter I would ever send to her. I wrote with a profound clarity—a clarity that allows you to feel so deeply you reach into the very depths of your being, and by doing so, you connect deeply with another. These have been the gifts that contemplating death bestowed upon me.

I've come to accept that discussing death is not a recognition of life's end but a celebration of its entirety and a call to urgency. It is a remarkable gift—one that illuminates not only the reality of our end but the beauty and the opportunity to act at any moment.

MEDITATIVE QUESTIONS

The Privilege of Reflection

How do you perceive the ability to reflect on death as a privilege? What circumstances in your life have allowed you this luxury, and how do they influence your perspective on mortality?

Lessons from Historical Figures

Reflect on Viktor Frankl's experiences and the teachings of Stoicism. How do these perspectives resonate with your own views on life and death? In what ways can you apply their principles to navigate your own relationship with mortality?

Impact of Reflection on Actions

Consider the story of my trip with Cees. How can reflecting on death prompt you to take actions you might otherwise postpone? What steps can you take now to ensure you are living in alignment with your deepest values and connections?

CHAPTER 7

Embracing the Vulnerability of Death

I HAVE SPENT much of my life sidestepping people's discomfort, avoiding topics that might bring them additional sadness or unease. It wasn't until recently that I realized I wasn't just avoiding their discomfort but my own. Discussing death often uncovers a deep vulnerability within us. It's a challenging topic, laden with emotional complexity, making open conversations about it rare and difficult. When I discuss death, particularly with my wife, the conversation inevitably turns to her aging parents, often bringing tears.

On one occasion, I began gently, "Hey, I know it's hard for you to think about saying goodbye to your parents."

Rani's eyes welled up with tears, and she looked away, trying to hold back the flood of emotions. 'It really is," she whispered. "I can't imagine life without them."

I reached out and took her hand, squeezing it gently. "I know," I said softly.

She bit her lip, her voice trembling. "Thinking about losing them makes me so sad."

"Yes," I said, feeling a lump form in my throat.

Rani nodded, tears spilling down her cheeks. "It's so hard to talk about."

We sat in silence for a moment, the weight of our shared sorrow hanging in the air. I gently wiped away one of her tears. "Maybe we don't have to say much. Just being here together, acknowledging it, is a start."

She squeezed my hand, her grip tight with fear and grief. "It's overwhelming."

"Thank you," she whispered, leaning into me.

I've made peace with these emotions within myself, which helps me discuss death, and the feelings that come with it. However, many people I interact with daily aren't able to do that yet. To start integrating discussions of death into our lives, we must first make peace with the intense emotions they stir up. Often, there's a profound sadness we haven't fully explored. If we shy away from our feelings, avoiding the vulnerability they evoke, we allow these unaddressed emotions to define us. This goes back to the saying, "What we resist, persists."

Writing about vulnerability is complex; it's not as simple as telling someone to "be vulnerable." See how well that goes over. You are more likely to experience more withdrawal. Instead, embracing vulnerability is more of a quiet and gentle journey into your subconscious. In my twenties, the mere mention of death would shut me down due to fear. Over time, as I cultivated a relationship with silence and introspection, I learned to sit with my discomfort, gradually making space for the underlying vulnerability.

It's common to struggle with opening up about death. You might feel isolated in your thoughts or fear judgment from others. For a long time, I believed I was alone in my contemplations of mortality. Eventually, I realized that many share these thoughts; I had just become more open about expressing them.

During a national tour to promote my first book, I facilitated sixty group sessions over three months. It was physically and emotionally exhausting. I invited participants to write a letter to a loved one as if it were their last. This exercise was inspired by the letter I sent my mother shortly before her death. Before each session, I resolved not to distance myself from my emotions, as I had for the previous 30 years.

I would begin each session with, "My mother was killed by a drunk driver when I was 18 years old, and that single moment changed my life forever." As these words left my mouth, I refused to let them become a mere concept—a habit I'd fallen into, allowing me to say the words without feeling their weight. Instead, I connected with the emotional meaning I had suppressed to protect myself. Inevitably, these words brought tears—sixty tear-filled sessions.

What I quickly learned was that by being okay with my own emotions, I was helping others feel safe to express their own.

When I failed to stay connected with my emotions, I saw the direct consequences. One of my initiatives was creating a board game titled "When My Time Comes," designed to help families discuss death through gameplay. The original version mixed light-hearted and more emotionally challenging questions, but I soon realized that the game required a facilitator to manage the intensity—it was more than just a game. Participants were often unprepared for the emotions that surfaced when the deeper, more challenging questions were asked. This experience taught me that individuals need to approach the topic of death in their own way and on their own timeline. Some may seem to handle it with ease, not necessarily because they're coping better, but perhaps because they've buried their emotions so deeply that they seem inaccessible, much like I had done for so many years.

I wish I could offer straightforward advice on how to approach vulnerability cautiously. But the truth is, vulnerability is inherently uncomfortable, revealing, and frightening. That's exactly what makes it so powerful. The essence of this chapter is to acknowledge that discussing death will invariably expose us to vulnerability, both our own and that of others. As challenging as it may be, it's important to recognize that understanding and embracing vulnerability is a personal journey, and we can't expect everyone to join or understand us on this path.

As we open ourselves up to our fears and uncertainties about death, we strengthen our connections with others and ourselves. Although it can make us feel exposed and uncertain, it also lays the groundwork for deeper emotional resilience and honesty in our relationships.

And, I do not want to be naïve to the fact that navigating our vulnerabilities can require more than just courage—but practical tools. Techniques such as mindfulness, reflective journaling, and structured dialogues, can help individuals process their feelings in a safe and constructive manner. Yet, you will see what makes sense for you, especially considering your cultural background and the limitations this may impose.

I embrace you as you navigate this journey and look forward to the day we might share these experiences in person.

MEDITATIVE QUESTIONS

Exploring Your Emotions

Reflect on a time when you felt deeply vulnerable discussing death or another challenging topic. How did you handle these emotions, and what did you learn from the experience?

Vulnerability in Relationships

How has your ability to discuss death and other difficult subjects influenced your relationships with others? What steps can you take to create a safe space for open and honest conversations?

Personal Barriers

What barriers prevent you from fully embracing vulnerability when discussing death? How can you begin to gently explore and address these barriers within yourself?

Death and the Law
of Attraction

ONE OF THE most intriguing aspects of writing a book about death is observing others' reactions when I mention it. I've encountered a spectrum of responses, from intrigued curiosity to outright discomfort. A common response has been, "Aren't you tempting fate by writing about death?"

This sentiment was epitomized during a conversation with a friend who is a renowned executive coach. Upon learning about my project, he exclaimed, nearly choking on his meal, "Why that subject? Why would you want to invite that into your life?" He suggested that every book he had written somehow manifested elements of its content into his life, implying I was inviting death by focusing on it.

Throughout the writing process, I've contemplated this idea. It amuses me to think that if I were to die during the writing, people might claim I had a premonition or brought it upon myself. Even those close to me have started expressing their love more frequently, preemptively mourning my absence.

Keeping an open mind, I acknowledge the possibility that this might indeed be my last book, an unintended invitation to my own end. Yet, I find this notion endearingly humorous because the true focus of my book is not on death itself but on learning to live with the awareness of death—a subtle but significant distinction.

My friend, the executive coach, further probed, "What are your thoughts on fate?"

Although I sensed his underlying beliefs influenced his question, I engaged with it and explained, "I see fate as a way to make sense of coincidences. Focusing on goals can certainly attract certain outcomes—like aspiring to be an executive coach might create opportunities through positive intentions. But where is the boundary between coincidence and fate? That depends on your beliefs."

He skeptically asked how this related to my book on death. I explained, "Writing this book has improved my mental state, clarified my thoughts, and deepened my interactions, making the overall experience profoundly positive."

Despite the curiosity about my focus on death, I find it odd that more people don't consider its implications more deeply. I'm not interested in dwelling on its morbid aspects or speculative questions like, "Is there life after death?" Instead, I'm intrigued by the clarity and urgency that the awareness of our finite time instills, and how the denial of this inevitability often paralyzes us with fear. As mentioned in a previous chapter, I take a more Stoic approach to the subject.

Discussing uncomfortable topics is naturally unnerving, and we often avoid them out of fear that addressing them might bring them closer to reality—as if by ignoring death, we can prevent it. However, I approach life differently. Rather than believing I craft my reality solely through focus, I believe that true living involves confronting our inner fears and doubts.

In my life, addressing the concept of death and my fears of eternal nonexistence has been essential for my development. Avoiding these fears only allowed them to fester and dominate my weaker moments. Now, as I enter my fifties and witness death becoming more prevalent around me, I see it not as a chance happening but as a part of life.

Facing death is indeed a delicate balance between confronting sadness and seizing the moment—carpe diem. Too much focus on the former can lead to depression, while solely pursuing pleasure might result in a lack of emotional depth.

Consider the archetype of the high-achiever, always on the chase for the next promotion, the bigger paycheck, the larger house. Their days are filled with meetings, their evenings with emails. To the outside world, they epitomize success, yet their relentless pursuit often leaves little room for deeper connections. Relationships are maintained for business purposes, valued for their utility rather than their emotional significance.

As years roll into decades, the facade of success builds, but so does the emotional vacuum. It's only as this high-achiever lies on their deathbed, the noise of ambition finally silenced, that the stark questions emerge: "What was the true value of my accomplishments? Did I truly live, or was I merely existing?" At this pivotal moment, the reflections aren't on the wealth accumulated but on the moments of genuine connection that were too often overlooked in favor of material gain.

This scenario underscores a poignant realization: life's richest experiences often don't come from what we achieve but from how deeply we connect with the world around us. The late realization on the deathbed—that no amount of success can substitute for profound human connections—serves as a powerful lesson. It highlights the importance of nurturing relationships and investing in people, not just financial portfolios.

Thus, the lesson here is clear. While ambition and achievement are not inherently negative, they must be balanced with efforts to forge meaningful relationships and make positive impacts on the lives of others. Doing so enriches our existence and ensures that when we reach our final moments, we can look back with satisfaction, not just at what we achieved, but at the love and legacy we leave behind.

Reflecting on my life, a significant moment comes to mind when those around me strongly believed in the idea that we attract what we focus on. After my mother's sudden passing, many people sought meaning in the timing of the letter I sent her just hours before her death. This remarkable coincidence sparked much speculation: Did I somehow intuitively sense what was about to happen? Was there a spiritual force at play, or did my act of writing influence the outcome?

I was sitting in my living room, the weight of my mother's passing still heavy on my mind, when my friend Sarah came by. She sat down beside me, her face etched with concern.

"I heard that you sent her a letter just hours before she died. That's quite a coincidence, isn't it?" she said softly.

I sighed, my thoughts drifting back to that fateful day. "Yes, it was."

"Do you think there was something more to it?" Sarah asked, her eyes searching mine. "Like maybe you sensed something was going to happen?"

I shrugged, feeling a familiar pang of uncertainty. "I've asked myself that question many times. Part of me wonders if there was some kind of intuition at play."

"It's almost like a spiritual force guided you to write that letter," she mused.

"I can see why you say that," I acknowledged. "The timing was just so uncanny."

These questions highlight our natural tendency to find significance in coincidences, though ultimately, they cannot be truly answered, much like the question of whether there is a Supreme Being. Rather than delving into mysticism, my key takeaway has always been the importance of seizing the moment to express my feelings while I still have the chance. I am grateful each day for that moment.

While I don't believe that discussing death invites it, embracing and accepting the inevitability of death has undoubtedly enriched my life. Recognizing that any interaction might be the last has made me more loving and empathetic, more attuned to the hidden struggles of those around me.

Therefore, our contemplation of death is not about speeding its approach but about deepening our appreciation of life. It serves to enrich our interactions and ensure that our moments, however fleeting, are filled with the deepest significance before they inevitably end.

MEDITATIVE QUESTIONS

Reactions to Discussing Death

How do you feel when the topic of death comes up in conversation? Reflect on why you might feel this way and what underlying beliefs or fears contribute to these feelings.

Tempting Fate

Have you ever worried that focusing on or discussing certain topics might "tempt fate"? How do you balance such concerns with the desire to confront and understand these important aspects of life?

Meaning in Coincidences

Reflect on any significant coincidences in your life that have made you ponder deeper meanings or spiritual influences. How do these experiences shape your understanding of fate and your actions?

CHAPTER 9

How Will I Be Remembered?

BEFORE MY FATHER died, he repeatedly asked, "Will you visit my grave?"

His voice carried a deep longing for reassurance that he wouldn't be forgotten, that his life had mattered, and that people would continue to honor his memory. Although I always affirmed that I would visit, his question always struck me as peculiar—not in his desire to be remembered, but in the notion that his essence could be confined to a cemetery plot.

In my view, I carry the essence of those I've lost within my heart, rendering a physical location seemingly unnecessary. However, I came to realize that a physical site provides a tangible space for existence beyond death—a place for visitation, albeit symbolic, that holds profound emotional significance as long as we collectively give it such meaning.

This idea is linked to our desire to persist beyond our physical demise, whether through familial memory or legal instruments like wills. This concept frequently arises in my work advising family wealth offices on crafting legacies.

If the term "legacy planning" is unfamiliar, it involves individuals with significant wealth deciding how to allocate their money after their death. Many realize that despite their riches, material possessions have their limits. Since wealth cannot follow them in death, their focus often shifts from accumulation to distribution—essentially, how to use their wealth to leave a lasting impact and be remembered.

Although I did not come from wealth, I had a strong desire to leave my own legacy. That journey began when I was 32 years old. I was utterly depressed in my work and terrified of making any serious changes. What I knew for certain was that my life felt meaningless. I was selling technology, products that were outdated mere months after purchase. Then, on one fateful day, I decided to change that. I sold all my possessions and moved to Amsterdam, embracing a simpler yet richer life under the guidance of my mentor, Cees.

For the three years prior to this transformative move, I often expressed my dissatisfaction with my life and my work. I repeated myself so often that I grew bored hearing my own complaints. Yet, I knew that merely changing jobs wouldn't alleviate the underlying emotional friction I felt. If I was truly to consider what I wanted my life to become, I needed to confront the deeper pain lingering from my childhood—the fear of death.

I kept this fear hidden from Cees during the first few months of our working together, until it surfaced unexpectedly in a conversation. I mentioned the word "God," and he responded with a dismissive tone, "You don't believe there is a God, do you?"

His tone left no room for discussion. To Cees, believing in God meant relinquishing agency to something unknowable. And if there was one thing about Cees, it was his belief that he could understand just about everything.

At that instant, I felt a chill run through me. Until then, I had avoided reflecting on this fear, worried that it might resurrect my childhood night terrors. I simply said, "I don't know." I also enjoyed leaving it as an open question, a source of comfort like the slim chance of winning the lottery.

In this new life I had chosen, I left myself little room for avoidance. I don't want to in any way suggest this was easy. My financial resources dwindled as I floundered to find my way. But, in spite of this, I found an incredible happiness—a sense of joy I had not felt since my childhood. And I have lived by the same motto ever since: "I will not do anything that does not bring me joy," and I have largely lived by that for the last twenty years.

Eighteen years later, this decision to shift my life took on a whole new meaning. On my 50th birthday, I found myself reflecting on my life and aspirations. Often, I've romanticized my existence as if I were sitting in the audience watching a movie about myself, wondering, "What is the character in the movie going to do next?"

The big idea came to me in the shower, clichéd as it may sound. I pondered, *What can I do to leave a lasting impact on the world while I'm here?* It wasn't just that I had the idea—it felt like the idea had taken hold of me, just as it had when I sold all of my possession and moved to Amsterdam. I rushed out of the shower, dripping wet, and found my wife, Rani, in the kitchen.

"Rani, I have an idea," I said, breathless with excitement. "I'm going to drive alone across the United States, asking people to write letters to their loved ones."

Rani looked up from the sink, a mix of curiosity and concern on her face. "Why? What brought this on?"

I took a deep breath, trying to gather my thoughts. "I've been thinking a lot about my life, about what I want my impact to be."

She set the dish she was cleaning down and gave me her full attention. "But why letters? Why this journey?"

"Because letters are so personal, so intimate," I explained. "They capture our thoughts, our emotions, our essence in a way that nothing else can. And this journey... it's about connecting with people, helping them express their feelings while they still have the chance."

Rani nodded slowly, her eyes softening with understanding. "So, it's about more than just the letters. It's your midlife crisis."

"I guess so," I said, feeling a surge of emotion. "I want to leave something behind that's real, that touches lives. Recognizing the inevitability of death has made me appreciate life so much more. I want to help others do the same, to deepen their appreciation for the people they love."

She reached out and took my hand. "I understand. Just promise me you'll be careful and come back home safely."

"I promise," I said, squeezing her hand. "This journey isn't just about me. It's about us, about leaving a legacy of love and connection."

She smiled, tears welling up in her eyes. "Then do it. Make that impact. Just know that I'll be here, waiting for you to come home."

Just months later, I was touring the US, driven by a surge of emotion and a deep-seated desire to make my life significant. I envisioned being remembered as someone who spread love, hoping my actions would be celebrated at my memorial with words like, "Andy loved so fervently that he had to share it."

And here's the crucial insight: I was driven by something so deep I didn't fully understand it at the time—a desire to somehow outlive my death. I was striving for my life to have meaning, blind to the inherent significance it already held. At that moment, I recognized that I wasn't so different from my father. He desired his name on a headstone; I sought mine in headlines. We both harbored a deep desire to be remembered, appreciated, and regarded as just and kind.

Reflecting on my father's struggles with his legacy, especially as he became estranged from many due to his manic outbursts, I've come to understand the importance of recognizing and valuing one's life contributions while still alive. His relentless questions about his legacy, even as his life waned, highlighted his unfulfilled search for meaning—a quest that ideally would have been pursued throughout his life, rather than in its twilight.

The day my father died, he was grappling with immense stress after losing all his money in a Ponzi scheme. He called me and my two brothers, one after the other. There was an urgency in his voice, as if he sensed his end was near, though he never explicitly said so. I believe it took his entire life to recognize the true legacy he had in his children. Even then, I don't think he fully appreciated the significance of that legacy. Burdened by strained relationships with us and having never found a meaningful way to share his wealth or time, he was left in solitude, haunted by a profound question: "What have I done with my life?"

He often asked me this question in the last days of his life, trying to make sense of his life in retrospect. Even sharing what his life had meant to me didn't help. He never identified his legacy as fatherhood. Seeing my father in those final days, it became clear to me that if you don't find the passion and purpose in life, you'll be left questioning it afterward. And I never felt that my father was ready to die. I believe he gave up the will to live, but he wasn't ready to die. He was still clinging to past regrets, stuck between living and waiting for a change that would never come—at least not before his death.

MEDITATIVE QUESTIONS

Legacy and Remembrance

Reflect on how you would like to be remembered. What legacy do you hope to leave behind for your loved ones and future generations?

Physical vs. Emotional Legacy

Consider the difference between a physical legacy (such as a grave or a monument) and an emotional or spiritual legacy (such as the impact you've had on others' lives). Which do you feel holds more significance for you, and why?

Reflecting on Life Choices

Look back on significant choices you've made in your life. How have these choices contributed to the person you are today and the legacy you are building? Are there changes you would like to make moving forward?

CHAPTER 10

How Can I Live Forever?

When I was a child, I remember being captivated by stories that Michael Jackson had plans to have his body frozen, betting on a future where eternal life would be scientifically possible. This fantastical tale was my first introduction to the concept of living beyond death outside the realm of traditional afterlife beliefs. It marked my initial encounter with the profound human desire to defy death. I recall wondering if, one day, it might even be possible for us to cure all sickness.

It was only recently that I revisited this intriguing concept. I was having a casual dinner with my friend Mark, when he suddenly brought up the topic of aging.

"Andy, you don't understand," he said with a gleam in his eye. "We can already reverse aging today."

I looked at him, my curiosity piqued. "What do you mean? How is that even possible?"

He leaned forward, clearly excited to explain. "Advancements in genetic engineering. Scientists are making incredible strides. They're working on ways to extend our lifespan indefinitely by altering the biological processes that lead to death."

I sipped my drink, processing his words. "That sounds like

something out of a science fiction novel. How do they plan to do that?"

"Well," Mark began, "there are a few different approaches. Some scientists are focusing on telomeres, the protective caps at the ends of our chromosomes that shorten as we age. By extending telomeres, they believe they can extend our lifespan."

I nodded, intrigued. "And what else?"

"Another approach is targeting senescent cells," he continued. "These are the cells that stop dividing and accumulate in our bodies, contributing to aging and disease. By removing these cells, researchers think they can improve health and longevity."

As his words got further and further away from my reality, and quite frankly my interest, I nodded and shifted to another topic. Not that the subject is not of great interest, just not one that I focus on in my life.

In a meeting with another friend, I was introduced to another aspect of holding on to life. But in this case, it was his idea for an app that facilitated interaction with the deceased rather than endeavoring to stay alive. Not as ghosts, but as digital remains.

"Andy, there's no reason you can't continue to interact with someone who's passed away, even many years later."

Somewhat naively, I asked, "How is that possible if they are gone?"

He smiled and pulled out his phone. "You see this? This device takes all the messages you've ever sent to someone and creates a digital fingerprint of your interactions, effectively mimicking past conversations."

Intrigued, I asked, "So, you're creating a persona based on your previous interactions?"

"You got it," he replied. "And that persona, using sophisticated algorithms and coding, does an impressive job of replicating the interactions you once had."

As I inquired why he hadn't proceeded with the product roll-out, I learned that unresolved ethical questions lingered. When I asked how he planned to address users potentially becoming too immersed in this virtual world, he mentioned considering a limit on the amount of time one could interact with a digitally immortalized person. Beyond the complexities my friend was navigating, our conversation highlighted our deep-seated yearning to escape death or maintain connections with those who have passed.

Odd as it may sound, this is just the beginning of what technology promises. With recent advancements in brain-computer interfaces, discussions are evolving toward digital immortality. Imagine a world where mind uploading allows the contents of one's mind to be transferred to a computer system, preserving consciousness beyond the physical lifespan. While this idea might seem like something out of a sci-fi movie, I've repeatedly heard a common refrain in Silicon Valley: "I am staying alive as long as I can so that I'll be able to click into immortality through technology that does not yet exist."

All of these conversations echo the cryonics discussions of my youth—a modern twist on the age-old hope to evade death. While some might see this as denial or escapism, I view it as an important cultural narrative that deserves understanding rather than judgment.

In my quest for understanding what is going on underneath all of these discussions, I often ask myself, *Why is this important to me?* Over and over again. Unraveling this question typically reveals deep-seated fears or desires, like layers of an onion. Consider a typical dialogue on this topic:

"Why do you want to upload your consciousness to a computer?"

"To ensure my thoughts and ideas persist beyond my death."

"And why is that important?"

"I want my insights to be carried on, even if my body is no longer functional."

"And why does that matter to you?"

"Because I want to be a benefit to society after I am gone."

"And why does that matter to you?"

"I don't like the idea of ceasing to exist."

"And what is behind that idea?"

"The terror of eternal nonexistence."

As Carl Jung famously noted, understanding these underlying motivations helps us bring what is unconscious into consciousness, preventing these unseen forces from directing our lives as though dictated by fate.

The desire to extend life beyond death is widespread, and understanding its origins can help us reconcile these feelings. I don't want to dismiss the technological advancements that prolong life or enable our digital selves to exist after death. However, it's crucial to recognize that we pursue these innovations for specific reasons. If we don't understand these motivations, we risk being driven by fear rather than inspired by life.

Dealing with our anxieties and fears about death is an intensely personal journey that lacks clear-cut answers. Yet, approaching this path with honesty and introspection shifts it from a mere escape from reality to a profound exploration of the self. While technology may extend our lifespans, focusing on making each day meaningful can enrich our lives immeasurably. Dwelling on the fears of tomorrow often stops us from fully embracing the joys of today.

MEDITATIVE QUESTIONS

Exploring Technological Immortality

How do you feel about the idea of technological advancements such as genetic engineering, cryonics, or mind uploading extending human life indefinitely? What are your thoughts on the ethical and emotional implications of these technologies?

Underlying Motivations

Reflect on your own reasons for wanting to extend life or preserve your legacy. What deep-seated fears or desires might be driving these thoughts? How can you bring these underlying motivations into your conscious awareness?

Balancing Fear and Inspiration

How can you balance the fear of death with the inspiration to live a meaningful life? What steps can you take to ensure that your actions are driven by a desire to embrace life rather than a fear of death?

CHAPTER 11

"Little Deaths" Throughout Life

THERE ARE TIMES in life when you search for a term to describe an experience, but none exists. In my forties, I coined the term "little deaths" to capture such moments. These "little deaths" were filled with such profound emotional loss that they resembled the pain of death itself. It was perplexing because, despite the overwhelming sadness and pain, the source of these emotions was difficult to identify. The pain felt disproportionate to the situation. For that reason, I also came to refer to this feeling as "ambiguous loss."

The first "little death" I remember was my high school graduation. High school was a formative time for me, it was where I built my social identity and experienced self-confidence for the first time. Saying farewell was deeply painful. Thoughts like "I will never experience this again," "This is an end," and "These friends are gone forever" dominated my mind. The intensity of these thoughts evoked the same feelings I associate with death—a sense of helplessness and permanence.

When I reflect on all the "little deaths" over the course of my life, the list is extensive: the end of significant relationships, the loss of jobs, financial insecurity, deteriorating health, relocating homes, and, something many can relate to, selling the home I grew up in. A particularly poignant example for parents is when a child leaves home, leaving them feeling as if a critical part of their life is over.

In a recent conversation, a friend whose last child had just left home shared, "Honestly, it's harder than I thought. I keep wandering into his room, expecting to see him there. And every time I realize he's not, it just hits me all over again."

I empathized, saying, "That sounds really tough. It's like you're grieving."

"It does feel like a sort of grief. I'm happy for him, really, I am. He's starting his own life, which is wonderful, but I just didn't expect to feel this loss so deeply," he admitted.

"You've spent so many years caring for them, and suddenly, your daily life changes completely," I noted.

"Yes, that's exactly it. My whole identity was wrapped up in being a dad, and now, I'm not sure what my role is anymore. It's like I've lost a part of myself," he reflected.

Beneath these "little deaths," I recognized a common thread: each was marked by a deep attachment to something I was reluctant to lose. Sometimes this attachment was to people whose absence would leave a massive void in my life, like a girlfriend or an office buddy. Other times, it was connected to experiences, such as selling my childhood home or leaving a beloved company. These were moments I found difficult to release, as the pain seemed disproportionate to the reality of the situation. I often felt like curling up in a ball and crying, but instead, I might shed just a tear, worried that sharing the depth of my actual pain would be viewed as exaggerated.

I remember the moment I came closest to fully experiencing one of these "little deaths." I was leaving Japan after living there for two years. In the days leading up to my departure, I found myself weeping daily. The weight of leaving behind a place that had become home, and people who had become family, was almost unbearable.

One evening, as my departure loomed ever closer, I sat down for one of my last dinners with my best friend, Hideki. The atmosphere was heavy with unspoken emotions. As we talked and reminisced about our time together, tears began to flow unexpectedly. At first, I tried to hold them back, but the dam broke, and I let the tears come.

Hideki, sitting across from me, didn't say a word. He didn't need to. Tears welled up in his eyes too, and soon we were both weeping, sharing a profound, unspoken understanding of the loss we were about to endure. At that moment, no words were necessary. The grief was tangible; it enveloped us, marking the end of a significant chapter in our lives.

Although it wasn't an actual death, the farewell carried the weight of finality. It marked the end of our chapter together. There was another example of such a loss, but in a very different context—the deterioration of the body.

In a recent conversation with a friend, he shared his struggles. "I've been feeling really down lately. It's like every day, there's something else I can't do anymore."

"I'm sorry to hear that," I replied. "It must be tough to face those changes."

"It's more than tough," he continued. "It feels like I'm losing parts of myself. Just last week, I realized I can no longer manage the stairs to my workshop. That was my sanctuary."

"That sounds incredibly hard," I responded. "Losing access to something that meant so much to you... I can only imagine."

"It's like every bit of independence I lose, I mourn it. It's not just the workshop. It's the little things, like not being able to open jars or tie my shoes. I never thought those things would matter so much," he explained.

"It's understandable to feel that way," I assured him. "Each of those things represents a part of your life, a part of who you are."

He nodded, "Exactly. And with each thing I can no longer do, I have to say goodbye to that part of my life. It's a series of losses, you know?"

In all of these discussions, one word has been mentioned a few times, but I want to take a moment to highlight its significance. Let's formally welcome "identity" into our conversations. This word has come to hold profound meaning in my life because it encapsulates so many of my daily reflections. One question I often ask myself is, *How is my way of seeing things so tied to my identity that I cannot even view it without bias? Can I ever truly know what that bias is?*

When I apply this to the aspect of saying goodbye to parts of ourselves, I realize that the hardest things to let go of are those most strongly attached to my identity. And just to be clear, this identity is who I believe myself to be, either consciously or unconsciously. For instance, if I say, "I am a great partner," it would be challenging for me to acknowledge that sometimes I am not a good partner because it is part of my identity.

No matter how many things I believe I've let go of, there always seems to be another aspect of my identity, another lingering attachment. For example, the pride I take in my career achievements, the sense of security from my financial stability, and even my self-image as a competent and reliable person are all deeply ingrained parts of who I am. Letting go of the notion that I must always succeed, or the idea that my worth is tied to my productivity, is incredibly challenging. And of course, there are identities that are core to who we are on the most fundamental of levels.

As I write this chapter, I am leaving Indonesia, where I visited my in-laws with my wife Rani. Although my own parents have passed away, Rani's parents are aging but still with us. Each farewell is laden with the heavy possibility that it might be the last, drawing deep tears from Rani as she confronts the painful reality that her parents will not always be part of her life. This impending loss is a significant part of her identity as a devoted daughter, a role with which she has not yet come to terms.

Throughout this process, I've noticed that the more Rani engages with the pain of her anticipated loss, the more loving and patient she becomes, both with herself and others. Conversely, when she distances herself from this pain, she tends to become easily agitated and frustrated, often saying things she later regrets.

Letting go is never easy, but as I often remind myself, avoiding it doesn't shield us from its consequences. Life presents a great paradox: by embracing pain, we open ourselves to joy. It is through accepting the pain of loss that we can truly appreciate and celebrate what we have now, no matter how ephemeral it may be.

Eckhart Tolle captures this beautifully with his words, "The secret of life is to 'die before you die' and find that there is no death." These "little deaths" are my practice runs. By learning to navigate each one, I am gradually preparing myself for my own eventual end, potentially realizing that I have metaphorically "died" before my actual death.

MEDITATIVE QUESTIONS

Experiencing "Little Deaths"

Reflect on a "little death" you have experienced, such as the end of a significant relationship or a major life transition. How did this experience affect you emotionally, and what did you learn from it?

Ambiguous Loss

How do you cope with feelings of ambiguous loss, where the source of pain is not easily identifiable or seems disproportionate to the situation? What strategies have you found helpful in managing these emotions?

Letting Go and Embracing Change

How do you handle the process of letting go, whether it's saying goodbye to a beloved place, a cherished role, or a familiar routine? What can you do to navigate these transitions with greater acceptance and peace?

Navigating Anticipated Loss

Reflect on a current or anticipated loss in your life. How can you prepare yourself emotionally for this loss, and how might engaging with the pain of this loss help you become more loving and patient with yourself and others?

CHAPTER 12

Romanticizing Death

AFTER MY MOTHER passed away, I spent years idealizing her life. I've observed the same pattern in others who have lost loved ones. We tend to glorify the positive aspects and overlook the negatives. For a long time, this perspective shaped my grief. I believed that experiencing profound pain was a way to keep my mother emotionally alive within me, memorializing her through my suffering. In doing so, I crafted an image of her that was so idealized, she became more of a caricature than the person she truly was.

I recall a conversation with a friend that opened my eyes to this. He pointed out, "Sometimes it seems like you put your mom on such a pedestal that it might be preventing you from seeing the full scope of your grief and emotions."

"It's just easier to focus on the good memories," I replied.

"I get that, but by only remembering her in a certain way, aren't you possibly denying yourself the full range of your feelings? Your grief might encompass more than just sadness—there could be anger or guilt, and that's perfectly okay," he suggested.

"I've never really thought about it that way," I admitted.

"And that's not wrong, but remembering her as a real person, flaws and all, might actually help you heal more fully. How do you really feel about everything?" he inquired.

"Honestly, I feel lost sometimes. It's like I'm clinging to this idealized version of her because confronting the reality that she's truly gone is too painful," I confessed.

This was the moment I began to see my mother for who she truly was. It wasn't until I could see her clearly that I would begin to truly understand myself. Why? Because by placing her on a saintly pedestal, I had unwittingly trapped myself. If I wasn't engulfed in sorrow, I would feel a wave of guilt. This state, often referred to as a "victim complex," is particularly challenging to navigate because it can become such a fundamental part of one's identity. I became emotionally attached to beliefs such as, "I will never feel uncon-ditional love again," and, "I lost the only home I ever had." These narratives obscured the real pain beneath them—the fear that I too would one day disappear.

Choosing not to romanticize my mother meant acknowledging her flaws. She was occasionally messy in her relationships, enjoyed her drinks, and often struggled to set healthy boundaries. She was human, and recognizing this allowed me to remember her as she truly was, not the idealized character I had created.

The intention was never to diminish my mother or lessen the gratitude I held for her. Instead, it was about making peace with another part of my identity. In doing so, my mind, once overrun with self-pity, began to quiet. I discovered that cultivating a serene mind reduced the pull of narratives that dragged me away from the present—whether you call it being centered, connected, or another term that resonates with you. In this tranquility, I found the ability to simply be with what is: the thoughts, the feelings, and the stories that emerge. Now, I no longer cling to these stories or reinforce them.

There are numerous ways people can fall into a victimization complex. Here are a few examples I've encountered regularly:

1. Career Stagnation: *John had been at his job for over a decade but was consistently passed over for promotions. Each time a less experienced colleague was promoted, John felt a deepening sense of injustice. He began to believe that the people in the office were working against him, and this belief colored his interactions at work. Instead of seeking feedback or ways to improve, he became increasingly resentful and disengaged, convinced that no matter what he did, he would always be overlooked.*

2. Relationship Struggles: *Lisa found herself repeatedly in relationships where she felt undervalued and unappreciated. After each breakup, she would tell her friends how she always ended up with partners who took her for granted. This narrative of being perpetually wronged by others became a central part of her identity, making it difficult for her to see her own patterns or take responsibility for her choices in relationships.*

3. Family Expectations: *Michael grew up in a family with high expectations, where success was measured by academic and professional achievements. Despite his efforts, he always felt he fell short of his parents' standards. As an adult, Michael internalized this disappointment, constantly feeling like a failure. He avoided pursuing his true passions, believing he was doomed to never meet his family's approval.*

4. Health Issues: *Sandra had struggled with chronic illness for years. While her condition was indeed challenging, she began to see herself solely through the lens of her illness. Every setback was met with a resigned, "This always happens to me," and she resisted exploring new treatments or lifestyle changes. Her identity became so entwined with her victimization by her illness that it prevented her from seeking ways to improve her situation.*

5. Social Injustice: *James grew up in a community that faced significant socio-economic challenges. Over time, he developed a deep-seated belief that the world was fundamentally unjust and that there was no point in trying to change his circumstances. This mindset led him to disengage from efforts to improve his life, viewing every obstacle as further evidence of a system rigged against him. His sense of victimhood became a barrier to seeing opportunities and taking proactive steps towards change.*

Reflecting on the narratives of victimization, it's clear how easily one can become ensnared by their own suffering. This identification with pain and loss leaves little room for deeper reflection. For years, I was caught in this very trap, but it was only through learning to release these self-limiting stories that I began to find true stillness.

This journey to stillness was not immediate. It required a conscious effort to detach from the narratives that had long defined my identity. I had to confront the fear and pain head-on rather than letting them shape my life. It was a slow, often painful process of unraveling the layers of grief and self-pity that had accumulated over the years.

In moments of quiet reflection, I started to see beyond the immediate pain. I began to explore what I call the "big black boxes behind the big black boxes"—the deeper, often hidden fears and questions about life and death that we all harbor. These aren't just existential musings; they are the core uncertainties that influence how we live our daily lives.

By embracing this expansiveness within myself, I opened up to a deeper connection with the world around me. Relationships became richer, experiences more vibrant, and even the smallest moments carried a profound significance. This peace was not a passive state but an active engagement with life, free from the constraints of old narratives and fears.

Clinging to an idealized version of an individual, and the possible stories that come from that, can keep us trapped in a loop of self-pity for years. At least that is how it was for me. I miss my mother, and my father, every day. Tears still come and go. However, what I no longer do is spin tales of what I've lost and what seems impossible in my life. By doing so, I created a reality that hindered the emergence of new beauty. In fact, through my wife Rani's love, I rediscovered unconditional love. Freed from the pain of the past, I welcomed love back into my life, embracing the possibilities of today.

MEDITATIVE QUESTIONS

Idealizing Memories

Reflect on how you remember your loved ones who have passed. Do you find yourself idealizing them or focusing only on the positive aspects of their lives? How does this affect your grieving process?

Acknowledging Imperfections

How can acknowledging the imperfections and complexities of your loved ones help you in your healing journey? What benefits might come from seeing them as whole, flawed individuals rather than idealized figures?

Victim Complex

Do you recognize any narratives in your life where you might be playing the victim? How do these stories shape your identity and interactions with others? What steps can you take to reframe these narratives in a more empowering way?

CHAPTER 13

The Cultural Context of Death

I CONSTANTLY QUESTION how much of my life has been influenced by how I was raised. Traveling has given me an incredible opportunity to see the world from many different perspectives. The country that had the most profound impact on me was Japan. I lived there for two years, learned the language, and somewhat integrated.

I say "somewhat" because anyone who has spent any time in Japan will attest to the fact that you never truly integrate as a foreigner. Yet, I came as close as I could. Part of that integration involved learning about their view of death. While working as a teaching assistant, the principal of that school passed away suddenly from a heart attack. Having never experienced death outside the US, I was unsure of what to expect.

I was shocked by the serenity of everyone's reaction. There was something indescribable about it. Although people were sad, there was an underlying acceptance that "things happen," similar to shrugging off a broken glass at home with a simple, "It's fine."

I do not want to downplay the pain people were experiencing, but there was a general acceptance that this is the natural process of life. I unexpectedly felt a sense of peace as I witnessed this cultural acceptance of the natural cycle of life, where death was not met with the dread I had experienced as a child.

During the year prior to this experience, I would visit friends' homes and see shrines in special alcoves created to honor their ancestors. Portraits of those ancestors encircled the living rooms, seeming to watch over us. Whenever I asked about the individuals in the photos, the reverence for the ancestors was evident, though few stories were shared. This contrasted with the American habit of recounting stories about deceased loved ones, often accompanied by tears. In Japan, it seemed they were already a seamless part of life, necessitating no additional stories or tears.

Each day, as incense was lit at the base of these shrines, a profound sadness and reverence were expressed—a daily tribute. There was something grounding about being in a society where death was embraced as a natural part of life. Gazing at the portraits of deceased relatives, I felt a reassuring calm, sensing the natural flow of life and death, and how these ancestors remained a part of their descendants' lives.

I was honored to be invited back to the home of the deceased principal to pay respects to his widow and participate in the funeral service. This experience puzzled me initially, as the colleagues at the school took significant responsibility for the arrangements, a contrast to my background where typically families, or church members, handle funeral details.

This active community participation underscored a key cultural difference I observed while moving between Eastern and Western cultures: the stark contrast between the West's fierce independence and the East's reverence for the group. Initially, this difference bewildered me. Being fiercely independent by nature, I found it challenging while living in Japan to adjust to what felt like sacrificing my own desires for the group's needs. My wife and I still discuss this daily, as she often reminds me to lower my voice on the street to avoid disturbing others.

Witnessing this communal sharing of death felt truly special.

I'm not implying that repressing emotions is a better way to cope, and there was certainly a fair amount of that. However, the deep, collective experience made it profoundly unique and meaningful.

Upon arriving at the principal's home, we bowed before his portrait in a brief, solemn ceremony marked by quiet and subtle communication—a stark contrast to more active Western expressions of grief that I had experienced.

During my stay in Japan, I was assigned a minder to help me settle in and avoid cultural misunderstandings. While at the home, he shared, "Your presence means a lot. We're preparing for the wake now, which is a significant part of our traditions."

"A wake?" I asked with a hint of wonder.

"Yes, it's called *otsuya*. We gather to keep vigil over the remains throughout the night. It's our way of providing company and comfort as the spirit starts its journey," he explained.

"That's beautiful. So, it's like you're guiding his spirit?" I said.

"Yes. Tomorrow, we'll have a Buddhist funeral service where the priest will chant *sutras*. These chants help cleanse the spirit and guide it towards peace," he continued.

"And after the funeral?" I inquired.

"We have the cremation, which symbolizes the release of the spirit from the physical world. During this, we perform a ritual where family members use chopsticks to transfer the bones to the urn. It's our final act of care and support for the journey," he replied.

"Using chopsticks to transfer bones... that sounds incredibly intimate," I said.

"It is. It's a way for us to be directly involved in the transition. Afterward, the urn is placed in the family grave, a sacred place where we can connect with the spirit," he explained.

"And you visit the grave?" I asked.

"Yes, especially during *Obon*, when we believe the spirits of our ancestors return to visit. We honor them with food, flowers, and prayers. It's a time to celebrate their presence in our lives, not just mourn their absence," he said.

"That's such a comforting thought, that they return and stay connected with you," I remarked.

"It is. It helps us to remember that death is not an end, but a continuation of their presence in a different form. This belief brings a lot of peace," he concluded.

In many ways, our relationship with death is not something we choose; it is passed down through tradition, education, and religion. It's difficult to gauge the extent of this influence and how it shapes the beliefs we think we've formed independently. Living in Japan allowed me to experience a completely different perspective on death, which, in turn, opened my eyes to my own socialization.

I realized that much of my fear of death stemmed from a sense of uniqueness and the desire to be remembered. This desire was deeply ingrained in me through my upbringing, fueling a longing to outlive my death, to achieve a form of immortality. In Japan, I encountered a different approach, one deeply connected to nature. The Japanese embrace both Buddhism and Shintoism, religions that honor the natural process of life. Instead of striving for immortality and recognition, there is an inherent humility and reverence for nature and ancestry.

Surrounded by this energy, I found myself less fearful of death. There was a sense of peace and tranquility, an acceptance of the natural process of dying.

My wife, Rani, is originally from Indonesia. She and I recently experienced the passing of a family relative on her side. When we expressed our sadness to her father, he looked puzzled and asked sincerely, "Why?"

His response wasn't dismissive but reflected a different perspective on death. He explained, "There is nothing to be sad about. She is back from where she came."

Hearing these words, a sense of calm washed over me, reigniting a realization I first encountered during my time in Japan. It was a profound reminder that I am part of something much larger than myself. The world does not revolve around me; rather, I am intricately connected to the vast expanse of the universe, linked in life and in death.

This deep understanding, that I first realized in Japan, has shown me how profoundly our upbringing shapes our views on nearly everything, including death.

MEDITATIVE QUESTIONS

Cultural Influences

How do you think your upbringing and cultural background have shaped your views on death and dying? Reflect on specific traditions or beliefs that have influenced your perspective.

Community and Grief

Reflect on the role of community in the grieving process. How does communal support differ in your culture compared to others you have encountered? How can you incorporate more communal elements into your approach to dealing with loss?

Rituals and Traditions

How do the rituals and traditions in your culture provide comfort and meaning during times of loss? Are there any practices from other cultures that you find particularly comforting or insightful?

Universal Connection

Reflect on the idea of being part of something larger than yourself, as mentioned in this chapter. How does this perspective influence your feelings about death and your place in the universe?

CHAPTER 14

Confronting the Terror of Insignificance

AT THE AGE of 24, I embarked on a year-long backpacking adventure around the world. About two months in, I traveled from Nepal to India. Coming from the affluence of the United States, the stark contrast in living standards was emotionally jarring. I had never before witnessed such poverty, malnutrition, and suffering. Each time I saw a child begging with a bloated stomach from starvation, my heart shattered.

A mix of emotions stirred deep within me, in the gray zone of my psyche that I referred to in previous chapters. The dark place where conflicting feelings merge into profound confusion. Guilt, sadness, helplessness, and frustration swirled within me.

Reflecting on the origins of these emotions, I am immediately transported back to my childhood. I remember the discomfort and sadness I felt upon seeing a homeless person. I struggled to comprehend how someone could survive on the streets and often feared, *What if that were me?*

These emotions were complex for a young mind, and they imprinted a sense of fragility and helplessness on my consciousness, which persisted into adulthood. Here, amidst such widespread suffering, I was pushing the boundaries of my emotional comfort.

Then came a life-changing event in Varanasi, a city on the Ganges River revered as Hinduism's holiest site. Here, Hindus perform rituals of bathing and spiritual cleansing, and it is also where the dead are cremated. Regrettably, some families, unable to afford cremation, place their deceased loved ones wrapped in cloth directly into the river.

I was in a small boat with a group of tourists when I noticed a small cloth floating in the water. Initially mistaking it for trash, we soon learned it was the body of a baby. My heart sank; I struggled to maintain composure and felt an overwhelming urge to vomit. I could not fathom that a human being could be treated with such disregard. There was a strange sense that this was not a piece of debris but a life once filled with potential and hope, now lost and forgotten.

At that moment, I was confronted with a thought that has never left me: how to come to terms with my utter insignificance in the grand scheme of things. Until that moment, I had a very self-centered view of the world. I believed that human lives were of utmost importance, and by extension, so was I. Seeing a human life so callously disregarded shattered that perspective.

Essentially, I am billions of times smaller than a microscopic speck on the back of an ant when compared to the vast cosmos. Adding to this dismaying thought is the realization that one day, even the sun will no longer exist. This left me grappling with the very real questions: *What purpose do I have here? Aren't we all taking this thing we call life just a bit too seriously?* I felt like I was turning into a character in a Woody Allen monologue, obsessing over the absurdity of existence and spiraling into an existential crisis, complete with neurotic musings about the meaninglessness of it all.

Throughout my adult life, I have wrestled with these profound feelings of insignificance. It is not my intent to diminish the marvels of human achievement, but rather to illuminate how frequently we fail to recognize our role within a grander design. I believe our struggle with insignificance is the root of many of humanity's greatest challenges—our relentless compulsion to build, to destroy, and to assert our worth.

It was 30 years later that I began to understand these feelings within a larger context. I was reading a small book on Existentialism, and halfway through, despite barely grasping the concept, I declared, "I'm an Existentialist!" This prompted a brief discussion with Rani, who humorously indulged my newfound fascination, curious whether it was merely a fleeting interest or something deeper.

Existentialism emerged post-World War II, during a period marred by the Holocaust—a stark demonstration of how trivially human life could be regarded. This philosophical movement posits that life inherently lacks meaning. However, it does not end there; if it did, existentialists would be nihilists. Instead, Existentialism asserts that we must individually ascribe meaning to our lives. This distinction is crucial, as even today, I have friends who mistakenly label me a nihilist. I saw Existentialism as a philosophy I was living but never openly discussing, fearing I might be labeled as negative, cynical, pessimistic, or even defeatist —labels not exactly fitting for a life coach.

In my work, I began to grapple with a significant challenge: the concept of finding "meaning" and "purpose." This idea, a staple for every aspiring life coach, clashed with my own definition. They spoke of life's destiny, while I emphasized making peace with the present. This day is all we have, make the most of it. They promised purpose and destiny as if it were an Easter egg hunt, whereas I was saying, we already have the egg. We were born. Now, how do we want to make each day meaningful? No destination. We are already there. Many people found this perspective perplexing, scratching their heads in confusion.

This perspective calls for adopting a humble view of ourselves, recognizing that we are part of something far greater. With this understanding, we have the potential to alter our behavior and reshape our concept of meaning and purpose. Contrary to the common fear that our lives would be stripped of significance, I believe this shift leads to a deeper sense of fulfillment. By stepping off the hamster wheel of chasing money, fame, or even the idea of a purposeful life, we can focus on our deepest desire—to feel connected to the present moment. This brings the joy of true contentment, found in appreciating and engaging with the here and now.

In the past, our identities were predetermined; a baker's child became a baker, a blacksmith's offspring followed suit. Today, we have the liberty to choose our paths, yet this freedom brings its own set of challenges and confusions. Underneath it all lies the implicit belief that life must have a purpose, a belief that remains largely unchallenged.

What if life genuinely lacks inherent purpose? Stated more directly, what if this is all just a cosmic accident, and there is no mysterious purpose to find? What if the notion of purpose is but a construct to lend significance to our existence? This thought is challenging and potentially alienating. Yet, accepting life's inherent meaninglessness doesn't strip it of significance. Instead, I've found that it enriches my existence, allowing me to cherish each moment as profoundly meaningful in its own right.

These moments—saying goodbye to my father for the last time, reflecting on my mother's final words, starting my life over at age thirty-five, expressing love to Rani, supporting a depressed friend—are the instants I treasure. By filling these moments with meaning, I am crafting a meaningful life, one day at a time.

As I write, I realize some readers might perceive contradictions with what I've written in earlier chapters, possibly even in this one. While I have no issue with contradictions, let me elaborate. When I describe actions that give my life purpose, such as driving across the U.S. on my Last Letter writing journey, those actions provided meaning and purpose at that specific moment. That was what I chose to do then, and now I've moved on to write this book. The journey continues to evolve, with different things arising on different days, and there are some months when I do "nothing." Even those months when I did nothing held significant meaning—sometimes even more than the accomplishments that look better on a life resume.

Finding meaning and purpose is a daily practice, not a quest for a final destination. It's in the small, personal actions: like helping my elderly neighbor carry her groceries, sharing a warm smile with a stranger on the street, or offering a listening ear to a friend in need. It's an ongoing process, and I embrace the fluidity of it, finding fulfillment in these everyday moments.

This brings me to a recent interview I had with Maria Shriver's Sunday Morning Paper. I was asked, ' How do you stay hopeful?"

I took a deep swallow as I was worried about what was about to come from my mouth. I replied, "You know, this might sound sad: I'm not hopeful. I could cry saying it. But I'm not going to let that stop me from being the loving, caring person that I would love others to be more of. It's not the hope that keeps me alive or going, it's the desire that I'm not going to succumb to everything else. It's not easy. I don't watch TV. I keep my influences very tight. If I'm around people with strong belief systems, I acknowledge them and appreciate them, but I don't defend or convince. I don't blame. So, in answering your question, I'm sadly not hopeful and yet, I don't let that stop me from being everything I want to be."

While the idea that our lives must have inherent meaning is common, realizing that we are part of a bigger story can be freeing and deeply satisfying. When we view life as shaped by the personal acts of love and the moments we cherish, it becomes not only bearable but also profoundly beautiful each day.

MEDITATIVE QUESTIONS

Grappling with Insignificance

Reflect on a time when you felt a profound sense of insignificance. How did this experience affect your perspective on life and your place in the world?

Finding Meaning in Existentialism

How do you relate to the existentialist idea that life lacks inherent meaning and it is up to us to create our own meaning? In what ways can this perspective help you live a more fulfilling life?

Balancing Purpose and Humility

Reflect on the balance between seeking a grand purpose and embracing the humility of being part of something larger than yourself. How can this balance bring more fulfillment to your life?

Creating Personal Significance

How can you create personal significance in your life through small, meaningful actions? Reflect on recent actions or moments that have brought you a sense of fulfillment and purpose.

CHAPTER 15

Do You Believe in God?

WHEN ASKED, "Is there a God?" I'm compelled to ask a question in return: "What makes that question important for you?"

It's not that the question itself is unimportant or irrelevant, but rather that I often find people's underlying reasons for asking it are missing from the conversation. The question can't be answered without invoking some belief.

In fact, when I'm asked if I am an atheist, I always respond, "No, because then I would need to believe in something." Namely, that there is no supreme being. The term given for people like me is "agnostic." Although this implies that I don't hold any specific belief, I've found that believers at either end of the spectrum often struggle to understand this worldview.

My relationship with God began early. My mother, the eldest of twelve Irish children raised on a farm in Carroll, Iowa, had a strong Catholic upbringing. It caused quite a stir when she married my Jewish father, particularly when she insisted on having her children baptized—a decision my father often reminded me "was not agreed upon ahead of time."

My brothers and I were sent to Catholic school, which gave me a sense of community despite my dislike for Sunday mass because

I couldn't sit still. While I struggled with the long services, I found joy in the tradition of picking up my favorite bagels afterward. This simple ritual became something I looked forward to each week.

Through these experiences, I began to see religion as filling the gap left by eternal questions like "Is there a God?" and "What is the meaning of life?" It felt like jumping on a train that already had passengers on it, offering a shared journey and a sense of direction.

With this sense of community came shared values and the deep human need for belonging. This need was so great that even serious shortcomings were often overlooked. For instance, when a priest was caught molesting altar boys, instead of being sent to prison, he was quietly shipped off to the Vatican. When my mother confronted the church on this matter, she was threatened with excommunication if she mentioned it to anyone. So much for living the values they preached.

Amidst this backdrop of religion, I began to formalize my relationship with God. I would pray frequently—praying to win in sports, for my mother's health, or even for nice weather. God became similar to Santa Claus for me; someone to whom I submitted my wish list and thanked when wishes came true, or dismissed when they did not. This relationship went unquestioned until the tragic day my mother was killed. That was the day I felt utterly betrayed by God, even blaming Him more than the woman who actually caused her death. Filled with anger, I started to rethink my relationship with God, transforming Him from Santa Claus to the Grim Reaper overnight. I use the word "Him" to refer to God because I come from a tradition that envisions Him as a figure in a white robe with a long white beard, looking down from the heavens.

It was not long after my mother's death that I began traveling the world, experiencing many religions I had never heard of before. There were billions of people following religions I knew little about, which led me to question: *How could it be that I just happened to be born in the one place that had the 'right religion'? How could a just God punish those who were unaware of its existence?*

After much reflection, I concluded that I didn't need to follow any prescribed religion or spiritual path. Instead, I could forge my own relationship based on personal values, though I recognized that even these were significantly shaped by Catholicism, particularly in attitudes toward sex where fear and shame were pervasive.

This leads back to the core of this chapter. Rather than asking if God exists, I find that exploring why we ask such questions leads to deeper insights. For me, acknowledging God's nonexistence meant never seeing my mother again—a thought so painful it pushed me toward wanting some form of religious belief. It also brought up fears of non-existence after death, compelling me to create beliefs to ease the anxiety.

To bridge this gap, I adopted the term "spirituality" to describe the blend of emotions that arose with thoughts of God. Saying, "I don't practice a religion, but I do feel myself to be spiritual," provided me with the breathing space I needed while I figured out how God fit into my life.

This reflection reminds me of a funny analogy involving two fish in a fishbowl.

One goldfish asks the other, "Do you think there is a god?"

The other goldfish confidently replies, "Of course, who else do you think feeds us twice a day?"

This playful story illustrates how our views are shaped by our own experiences and how challenging it can be to find clear answers to life's big questions—questions that we often try to answer from the limits of our own perspectives.

What I have come to understand is that there is always something beyond my comprehension, something outside the reach of my senses. Acknowledging this has brought humility and a sense of wonder. As I observe this wonder, I sometimes feel hope seep through, prompting me to slow down and examine my feelings. In these moments of quiet observation, I feel closer to a higher power—a connection not easily labeled as God, oneness, or anything mystical, as such labels might detract from the genuineness of the experience.

In sum, discussing whether God exists can lead to confusion and disconnection, especially when one person's experiences may not align with another's. Each of us has our own journey and relationship with what might be called God, and this relationship is deeply personal. Rather than convincing others of its validity, it is more about tuning into our own unique frequency—finding the "God frequency" in ourselves. This is why I avoid defining this connection with definitive terms. Instead, I focus on the personal, the immediate experience of being connected, which for me, feels like embracing a warm, inner light—a sentiment echoed throughout this book.

If directly asked whether I believe in God, my answer would be, "No, which also does not mean that I disbelieve." Belief distracts me from experiencing. When I am connected, I am not thinking of a God; I am experiencing divinity within myself, embodying my father's provocative assertion, "I am God." This does not mean I consider myself divine, but rather that we each carry a divine spark within us. Finding and tuning into this frequency is a personal journey, one that does not require external validation or agreement.

Thus, does God exist? What compels you to ask?

MEDITATIVE QUESTIONS

Personal Motivation

What compels you to ask whether God exists? Reflect on the deeper reasons behind your curiosity or belief. How do these reasons shape your spiritual journey?

Personal Connection

How do you connect with what you might call a higher power or divine presence? What practices or moments help you feel this connection most deeply?

Exploring Beyond Belief

How can you explore your spirituality or connection to the divine beyond the confines of belief? What practices can help you experience this connection more authentically and personally?

CHAPTER 16

Reincarnation, Control, and Surrender

My original intention was to write separate sections for each of the three words that form this chapter's title. However, as I delved deeper, I found it impossible to separate them because, in my mind, they're all interconnected.

My relationship with reincarnation has significantly evolved over the years. A friend insightfully remarked, "Reincarnation is our way of dealing with the remorse for all the things we've been unable to resolve in our lifetime." The idea is that, with another life, we have the chance to address the unresolved issues from this one.

Every day in my coaching practice, I encounter the concept of deferring life's challenges. I often witness the immense guilt individuals feel from avoiding issues, sometimes for decades. This is especially true for complex matters involving families and life partners.

I've observed that reincarnation exists in a delicate balance between control and surrender. The notion of surrendering to death is unsettling, prompting us to cling to control in various ways, such as meticulously planning our futures, obsessing over health and wellness, or maintaining rigid routines. Yet, in doing so, we fail to see how this fear prevents us from fully living in the present moment, as discussed throughout this book.

As acceptance grows that we cannot control everything about our lives—as much as many would prefer—we transition from control to surrender. Surrender is more than just a concept; it's a tangible experience characterized by relaxation in the body, softness in the voice, and an overarching sense that life's challenges are manageable.

This isn't merely about intellectual understanding; it's about embodying a state of being. In surrender, we observe the world passing by without trying to influence the outcome or dictate how things "should" be. We allow life to unfold naturally.

Control, on the other hand, manifests when we feel helpless, which can be seen most clearly in financial matters. Throughout my life, my father wielded money as a means of control, using threats of disinheritance to shape my behavior. This approach invariably alienated me, leading to a decade-long estrangement from him.

This theme of controlling financial legacies is prevalent among many of the individuals I work with, particularly those from wealthy backgrounds. They grapple with questions like how much to leave their children and how to ensure the money is spent wisely. Concerns about potential misuse lead to "controlling from the grave," where detailed conditions are set to ensure responsible spending.

This brings us to the counterpoint of control, which, as I mentioned, is surrender. This, in turn, brings me to my childhood friend Mark. We were best friends in grade school, and although our interests have not always aligned, our friendship has never wavered. I seldom discuss my work with him, as I see him gaze back at me with a look that resembles constipation. But when I mentioned this book, he remarked, "Andy, you know that death is ultimately about losing control, which is deeply unsettling."

His observation made me smile, appreciating both his insight and this rare engagement with my writing. Mark highlighted what

I consider the ultimate relinquishment of control: death. Once I am dead and gone, I cannot direct or influence; I am utterly absent from the proceedings.

This presents a critical choice: Do I spend my life attempting to control the future, including that of those around me, or do I choose to surrender?

Surrender does not imply indifference but rather a peaceful acceptance of life's processes. It involves expressing preferences without insisting on strict adherence to them, understanding that circumstances may change after one's departure.

I've discovered that surrender often unfolds naturally as life progresses. This realization struck me most profoundly while being with friends in their final moments; there comes a time when there is nothing left to say—just a sense that it's time. I hope to embrace such surrender not only at life's end but as a peaceful acceptance throughout life.

One of my friends, Phyllis, was among the first to join me on my podcast. She was navigating her third battle with cancer and hinted that it might be our last time together, though she barely mentioned it during our talk. Just a few days later, she ended her life, ingesting a lethal cocktail in a ceremony with her friends surrounding her. The pains had grown too great. Her final words to me were, "Don't be afraid. Don't be afraid. I look forward to it."

Those words have stayed with me ever since. She had surrendered so completely that I didn't detect an ounce of resistance. I was, and continue to be, deeply inspired by her. Her unwavering courage in the face of death reminds me of the Stoic virtues. Phyllis was a role model for us all.

In my life, I've opted to surrender in most situations. This doesn't mean I lack interest or involvement; rather, I prepare thoroughly and let events unfold as they will. This approach has often led me further than I could have imagined, whereas pushing for specific outcomes has seldom been fruitful.

My hope for you is that you find peace in surrender. It's not always easy—there are desires and goals we all strive to achieve. Yet, true internal peace requires surrender, accepting that we cannot control every outcome. If that proves challenging, we can always consider the concept of reincarnation, allowing us the comfort of potentially addressing today's challenges in another life.

MEDITATIVE QUESTIONS

Concept of Reincarnation

How does the idea of reincarnation resonate with you? Does it provide comfort or raise questions about how you address unresolved issues in this life?

Balancing Control and Surrender

Reflect on areas in your life where you exert control. How does this control impact your ability to live in the present moment? How can you begin to practice surrender in these areas?

Experiencing Surrender

Describe a time when you felt a deep sense of surrender. What were the circumstances, and how did it affect your emotional and physical state?

Learning from Others

Reflect on someone you know who has embodied the virtue of surrender in their life. What can you learn from their example, and how can you apply those lessons to your own journey?

CHAPTER 17

Death and Sex

I HAVE OFTEN sensed a profound connection between my fear of death and my sexual drive. When existential fear arises, it's as if a chemical surge activates within me. Though this relationship has never been entirely clear to me, I can attest to its presence in my life. In my quest to understand this, I discovered that existential philosophers Jean-Paul Sartre and Albert Camus believed that our fear of death and sexual desires are closely linked to our search for meaning in life.

Both Sartre and Camus explored the inherent absurdity and meaninglessness of life, especially in the bleak aftermath of the Holocaust. The feelings arising from such an emotion are what we now refer to as existential dread. This is the same feeling that arose within me as a child and still lingers during my moments of deepest helplessness today. According to these philosophers, sexuality was a way to assert one's existence and find temporary relief from the terror of meaninglessness. The sexual act provided moments of transcendence and connection that temporarily alleviated existential concerns. Sartre believed that confronting this anxiety head-on was essential for authentic living. He emphasized that by acknowledging our mortality, we could transcend our fear and live more genuinely.

In my case, I have observed this pattern unfold predictably. Exposure to news of war or environmental catastrophe triggers childhood fears and a deep-seated anxiety. This is closely followed by a compelling urge that feels almost self-destructive. The sensation is what I associate with addiction—a profound loneliness accompanied by an intense longing to feel alive and challenge the limits of existence. These are not emotions that I can easily define; they stem from a darker, more primal part of myself. It feels like an underdeveloped child lurking in the shadowy recesses of my mind, unseen and desperate to act out.

I vividly recall the despair I felt when the Twin Towers fell on 9/11—a stark reminder that the world could indeed end, heightening my fear and helplessness. During this time, I found myself looking for meaningless sex and visiting brothels in Vienna, engaging in an existential struggle to feel alive. Entering the brothel, I felt an electrifying intensity, rebelling against societal norms and pushing back against the world in a profound act of defiance. This experience echoed the themes described by Sartre and Camus, who explored how confronting the absurdity and meaninglessness of life can lead to actions that defy societal expectations.

Research supports the complex interplay between danger and desire. For instance, a 1992 study revealed that approximately 17 percent of surveyed U.S. soldiers believed the risks associated with unprotected sex, even with the potential for contracting AIDS, were worth taking.[1] This was at a time when AIDS was still incurable. Similarly, Planned Parenthood has recounted stories of teenage girls, trying to prove their resilience, engaging in unprotected sex with HIV-positive gang members.[2] These examples illustrate how the allure of sexual desire can be magnified by its taboo nature, transforming risky behaviors into acts of defiance. Such scenarios

---

1 Source: https://www.ncbi.nlm.nih.gov/books/NBK218623/

2 Source: https://www.chicagotribune.com/news/ct-xpm-1993-04-26-9304270152-story.html

underscore the intense and often irrational human response to forbidden temptations.

The experience mirrored the heart-racing terror of my childhood night terrors—surprisingly similar feelings tied to vastly different experiences. In some ways, challenging these boundaries felt like a rebellion against my past, providing a fleeting sense of being vibrantly alive. However, this aliveness was fleeting. Leaving the brothel, I would plunge into even greater sadness and depression, spending hours brooding over global destruction and the inevitable demise of the planet.

Beneath it all lay a deep-seated fear of death, though I could not have identified it at the time. The gray zone of my brain, that I have mentioned throughout this book, was active, elusive, and beyond my straightforward understanding. All of my existential fear and the compulsion to engage in risky sexual behavior was inside this box. I have accepted that this part of my brain is very deeply wired, a section of my psyche that I can feel but not logically explain. This is the realm I associate with addiction, an overpowering need that must be quenched, albeit not through substances but through behavior that risks self-destruction.

Navigating this gray zone has taught me humility and helped me recognize that there is a part of our psyche beyond rational comprehension. In my coaching practice, I distinguish between higher-order thinking, like decision-making and goal-setting, and the irrational compulsions of addiction, which cannot be engaged with conventional rationality. This interplay between death and sexual desire was also reflected in Sigmund Freud's assertion that life's two primary drives are to reproduce and to avoid death, subjects often considered too taboo for polite conversation.

Today, I no longer see these urges as taboos to be suppressed, as my Catholic upbringing might suggest, but rather as natural emotions. Living in Amsterdam, where sex work is normalized, I regularly pass by the red-light district. This environment has provided a unique perspective, allowing me to confront and reassess my internal taboos, and truly feel the intensity of these urges.

This transition has led me from experiencing life as a series of reactive events driven by external stimuli to embracing a more spiritual existence. The gray zone, once a source of turmoil, has become a gateway to deeper insights. By observing how external influences impact me, I foster a greater understanding of myself and, by extension, the human condition.

MEDITATIVE QUESTIONS

Existential Dread and Sexuality

Reflect on the concept of existential dread as discussed by Sartre and Camus. How do moments of fear and anxiety influence your behaviors and desires?

Risky Behaviors and Defiance

Have you ever engaged in behaviors that felt defiant or self-destructive in response to feelings of helplessness or fear? How did these actions impact your sense of self and your emotional well-being?

Understanding the Gray Zone

Reflect on your own "gray zone"—that part of your psyche that feels beyond rational comprehension. How do you navigate this space, and what have you learned from it?

The End of the World

HUMANITY HAS ALWAYS been fixated on the end of the world. The theme is often amplified by media outlets to boost ratings. This preoccupation is evident in the daily bombardment of messages heralding the planet's demise. While the word "death" is rarely used explicitly, nearly every story evokes the associated emotions. Instead, terms like "climate crisis" dominate the narrative.

I recognize that the topic of a climate crisis can incite intense reactions, but my intention here is not to delve into that debate. Rather, I aim to explore the existential dismay that surfaces whenever this subject is raised. It reminds me of the ominous feelings that arise when a loved one is diagnosed with cancer. We sense that death is looming, but we cannot be sure how much time we have left, in this case, regarding human existence.

Acknowledging that this topic can be profoundly unsettling, I don't raise it merely to stir discomfort but to delve into something much more compelling: our internal processing of these frightening thoughts. You may notice a visceral reaction when confronting terms like "human extinction," "nuclear war," or "climate change." While not everyone experiences this, for me personally, the thought of the world ending invokes profound fear. It taps into my deepest fears, where emotionally charged thoughts cause physical reactions like a tightening throat and a general sense of unease.

I regularly meet my friend Francesca in the park for a walk, and one day, she told me, "I've been feeling really anxious lately, and I think it stems from thoughts I've had since I was young."

"Tell me," I responded.

"When I think about the extinction of the human race, I feel this overwhelming fear," she explained. "Even as a child, the idea of the world ending terrified me."

"I understand," I said gently. "Those are deeply unsettling thoughts."

"It's not just a mental thing," she continued, her voice shaking slightly. "I feel it physically too. My chest tightens, and I sometimes have trouble breathing. It can impact an entire day."

"That sounds horrible," I said, nodding. "How do you process it?"

"It helps to talk about it," she admitted. "But why does it feel so intense?"

"It appears that your body is reacting to your mind's fears," I explained. "Even when there's no immediate threat, emotionally charged thoughts can cause physical reactions."

"That makes sense," she said, her expression softening. "I feel so incapacitated when my fear and anxiety impact me so much."

"Acknowledging them is the first step," I replied.

This exchange underscores the powerful associations that some topics, such as death, have on us—they can completely consume our emotional state. I've observed that consuming negative news tends to activate my limbic system, plunging it into a state of heightened fear. I mention this because contemplating the planet's extinction can trigger our deepest fears, questioning the very continuity of our existence and that of future generations.

This topic is vast, and I want to focus on two key points. The first is acceptance, which may seem callous, but it's the only way I can frame it. Living in constant fear of human extinction can be paralyzing. One could argue that living with such fear might even hasten one's death. Tragically, I have witnessed people so overwhelmed by guilt for merely existing, perceiving themselves as burdens to the planet, that they sometimes choose to end their lives.

The concept I advocate is radical acceptance, which I discussed earlier in this book. While explaining this, I anticipate some readers might protest, "You shouldn't downplay the impact of human activity on the earth."

My intention is not to diminish this impact but to encourage personal reflection on how this perception influences individual behavior and mental health. Being unable to make peace with the future demise of the planet is no different than being unable to make peace with our own demise. Both are deeply rooted in our attachment to continue existing. There is a sense of pain that is so deep that it stops us from sitting still and being present to our own emotions.

Hence, as I've mentioned, radical acceptance has become my method to soothe the relentless fears within me. I affirm to myself: "The world will one day end, and that's okay." "The human race will eventually become extinct, and that's okay." "One day, I will cease to exist, and that's okay." This approach helps me find peace with the inevitable, allowing me to live more fully in the present.

I voice these affirmations to quiet the incessant chatter in my mind, enabling me to regain presence in the current moment. Whenever I neglect to address my fears and sidestep them instead, they end up shaping who I am. This pattern dates back to my childhood, where the fear of discussing my worries molded my identity. By not confronting these fears, I have inadvertently allowed them to evolve into complex adult anxieties. Yet, at their core, they stem from the same foundational fear lurking in the gray zone of my consciousness.

I often wonder if my anxiety is more about the fear of experiencing a catastrophe firsthand or the helplessness of watching a disaster unfold, like a train speeding toward a cliff with no way to stop it. Discussing these fears is important because it helps us understand how external events affect our minds and bring unconscious thoughts to the surface. This ties back to the previous chapter and the question about God's existence: "Why do you ask?" By slowing down my reactions, I've realized that these apocalyptic thoughts mirror the night terrors of my childhood, invoking a deep sense of helplessness. Making these unconscious thoughts conscious allows me to hold space for those frightened and vulnerable parts of myself.

This segues into another recurrent theme in my life and arguably one of the most challenging emotions I've grappled with: helplessness. It's the sensation that no matter my efforts, they are insufficient to effect the change I hope for. This can easily lead to apathy and pessimism. I do my best to avoid these pitfalls, though it's not always easy. Paradoxically, I rely on the tool of radical acceptance, no matter how difficult it may be. I find myself grappling with the question, "How can it be okay that the planet will end?" This ongoing internal dialogue is not just philosophical but deeply emotional, pushing me to find peace with the inevitable and to embrace life's transience.

With deeper insight, we can see that the natural cycles of ebb and flow are essential to our human experience, even if we often fear embracing them. Despite the difficulty in accepting it, we are merely a part of the broader rhythms of life. Humanity did not exist for billions of years before us, and it's likely we won't exist for billions more. This truth can be tough to accept, but it is an inherent aspect of life.

Embracing this reality allows us to live in the present without being overwhelmed by the sensationalized news and media that pull us away from our emotional centers. We are granted the extraordinary chance to experience life fully, embracing all of our senses. This acceptance doesn't mean we trivialize our emotions; rather, it means we appreciate life's impermanence and value the present moment even more.

We can live a fulfilling life, even as we're aware that the planet is continually evolving and that one day, conditions here may no longer support human life. This fact shouldn't paralyze us with fear; instead, it should inspire us to live with greater purpose, urgency, and kindness. Recognizing our transience can become a powerful motivator for positive change.

In accepting the uncertain future of our planet, we are not excused from acting responsibly to support it. Some friends who label me a nihilist often assume that this means I don't care about my surroundings or the future. Far from it. Acknowledging our finite time here gives us the opportunity to embrace life fully and become even more conscious of how we treat our planet during our short time here.

MEDITATIVE QUESTIONS

Emotional Reactions to Global Events

How do news of global events, such as climate change or potential nuclear threats, affect your emotional state and behavior? Can you identify any patterns in how you respond to these triggers?

Radical Acceptance

Reflect on the concept of radical acceptance as discussed in this chapter. How do you feel about accepting the eventual end of the world or human extinction?

Embracing Transience

How do you reconcile the impermanence of life with your daily actions and decisions? In what ways can acknowledging our transience inspire you to live with greater purpose and urgency?

CHAPTER 19

Understanding and Accepting Suicide

THROUGHOUT MY LIFE, several friends have chosen to end their lives. Witnessing these loved ones disappear has profoundly affected me and reshaped my understanding of suicide.

The first was Jason, who took his own life due to financial despair. When I received the news, a profound sadness consumed me, deeper than the sorrow of losing a friend. It was compounded by a nagging guilt—a feeling that perhaps I could have intervened, or that there were warning signs I had overlooked. I found that my thoughts frequently centered around "I": what I could have done differently, what I might have said, how I might have supported him. This self-focused reflection made me feel, in some ways, responsible for his death, as if I could have prevented it by being more proactive.

I soon realized that this self-centered approach to processing grief was unproductive. What I lacked was true compassion for my friend.

Over time, my perspective on suicide has profoundly changed. I no longer view it simply as the end of life but rather as the end of unbearable suffering. This understanding is complex, especially within a society that heavily stigmatizes suicide as unequivocally negative. Yet, having grappled with suicidal thoughts myself, I recognize that for some, the decision to end their suffering is a deeply personal choice.

For instance, a close friend suffering from terminal cancer expressed a wish to end her life on her own terms rather than endure prolonged agony. She hesitated, not wanting "suicide" listed as her cause of death—a reflection of societal stigma. Ultimately, she couldn't fulfill her wish to travel to a place where euthanasia is legal and suffered until her natural death. This and similar experiences have shaped my understanding that individuals who choose suicide are often trying to escape unbearable pain rather than life itself.

In my journey of writing this book, I recently encountered the profound complexity of human suffering through my dear friend Will. Will confided in me about his intention to end his life, marking a date that was symbolically significant as it was the anniversary of his father's death. Our weekly discussions were not just mere exchanges of words, but deep dives into the essence of existence and the haunting echo of purposelessness that he felt.

"Andy," he once said, "the party ended for me many years ago. I don't know why I'm still here."

When Will read the draft of this chapter, he pointed out a crucial missing piece—a perspective that I had completely overlooked: the profound sense of relentless boredom.

"What if you are just bored?" he questioned.

This was a pivotal moment for me; it was a perspective that was as unsettling as it was real. His boredom was not of the mundane kind but a deeper, existential weariness—a soul tired of being.

Despite my attempts to infuse hope or redirect his path, I realized that any form of encouragement unwittingly accelerated his resolve. It was a delicate balance, trying to be present for someone who sees no future ahead. Eventually, Will chose to depart this world a few months earlier than he had initially planned, leaving me in a swirl of emotions. I was torn between the grief of losing a cherished friend and a somber relief that he found his peace, his escape from an unbearable existence.

In grappling with Will's decision, I've come to understand the immense power of compassion over judgment. Viewing his choice through a lens of compassion, I see not a selfish act, but the end of an unbearable suffering—a decision made not out of haste but from a place of profound personal truth.

I can hear the concerns of some skeptical readers: "If you downplay the sanctity of life, aren't you making it easier for people to justify ending their lives? That can't be good."

This thought leaves me with a heavy heart. Indeed, some individuals battle mental illness, and with adequate, sustained support, they might find a more stable footing. The prevailing idea is that time can heal the impulse towards suicide. This recalls an incident involving a college friend who, overwhelmed with shame after being caught shoplifting, chose to end his life by jumping in front of a train rather than confront his embarrassment.

In such scenarios, I firmly believe that helping individuals regain their footing can significantly alter the outcome, transforming a rash decision into a more considered one.

I had another friend who composed a suicide note one evening and set it to send the following morning. He meticulously informed a few close people of his irreversible decision to end his life. His message was clear and deliberate: "I'm tired of suffering, and this is a choice I have made. There was nothing you could have done to help me." He outlined his reasons for his decision and left specific instructions for those who would find him.

I share these details to underscore that I do not advocate strict rules about suicide; instead, I aim to foster open dialogue. Labeling suicide categorically as wrong can be restrictive and may prevent individuals from fully considering their personal circumstances and needs. Such judgment does not accommodate their agency or the thoughtful conclusions they may have reached on their own. In this context, holding space for someone means supporting them through their challenges without judgment or imposing expectations.

This brings me to a broader reflection on compassion in my life. If I prioritize understanding over judgment, if I can acknowledge the profound suffering of another without superimposing my own beliefs, how might that transform my perspective? This approach doesn't necessarily mean condoning all decisions, but it does mean trying to understand them within the context of what someone is enduring. This recognition challenges us to consider compassion over condemnation, inviting a deeper more empathetic engagement with the complexities of human suffering.

In my experience, cultivating genuine compassion for someone becomes exceedingly challenging when we fundamentally oppose their perspective as inherently wrong. Common societal assertions like "Life is sacred," "Suicide is a sin," or "Only weak-minded people commit suicide," can deeply influence our ability to empathize.

When supporting someone with suicidal thoughts, I approach with deep compassion for their pain, while recognizing the profound helplessness in not being able to make decisions for them. I do offer reassurance that their current distress might lessen with time and provide compelling reasons to continue living. However, ultimately, the decision is theirs, not mine.

The profound sense of helplessness associated with suicide surpasses any other type of death I've encountered. This became starkly evident during my tour across the United States, where I invited people to pen their "last letters." A recurring sentiment in letters addressed to those who had committed suicide was a heart-wrenching regret: "I could have done something. I should have done something," much like the experience I had with my friend Jason.

These expressions of remorse highlighted the deep impact of suicide on those left behind, reinforcing the complex layers of grief and responsibility we often feel. This underscores the "I" processing of suicide, where personal reflection and regret add to the burden of grief.

Suicide is undoubtedly one of the most challenging subjects to discuss due to its emotional depth and complexity. It requires a careful balance of empathy, understanding, and respect for individual autonomy. By shifting our perspective from judgment to compassion, we can support those grappling with these difficult decisions and perhaps ease some of the associated societal pressures.

From the moment we are born, we begin the process of dying. What if we were more accepting of that process? What would it mean for how we think about suicide?

MEDITATIVE QUESTIONS

Self-Focused Grief and Compassion

How do you process grief when you lose a loved one to suicide? Do you find yourself focusing on what you could have done differently? How might shifting this focus to compassion for the individual help in your grieving process?

Societal Stigma and Personal Choice

How do societal stigmas around suicide influence your views on the subject? Have you noticed any shifts in your understanding when considering the personal choice aspect of suicide?

The Complexity of Human Suffering

How do you navigate the complexity of understanding and accepting someone's decision to end their life? What role does empathy play in this process for you?

Accepting the Process of Dying

Consider the idea that from the moment we are born, we begin the process of dying. How might accepting this natural process influence your views on suicide and the end of life?

CHAPTER 20

Transcending the Fear of Death

In June 2019, during a visit with a friend, I found myself on the cusp of a profound experience—turning fifty. I had never before ventured into mind-altering substances, except for marijuana, which merely made me sleepy. As we relaxed on the back deck of the house, my friend Sam, well-versed in psychedelics, eagerly suggested I try DMT. I had already emotionally decided to give it a shot, but not said it out loud, as I wanted to let the night unfold and feel when the moment was right for me.

When I reflect on why I'd never taken mind-altering substances until this point in my life, the answer shoots up in me without reservation: because I was scared to. My reluctance to explore mind-altering substances stemmed from fear, a residue from childhood warnings about their dangers, like the tale of someone thinking they could fly and jumping out a window. A story that touched me personally when a friend did just that. The thought that I might do something that would kill me outweighed any gain I might receive.

As we sat around the table discussing, Sam became more and more insistent, "You've got to do it. You've got to have this experience."

Although I could see that his intentions came from a very loving place, I felt pushed and I could feel my anxiety rise. I knew he would continue to push if I did not reveal my intentions. So I said, "Sam, I have already decided to try. You can relax now. I just wanted the night to unfold and see when it felt comfortable."

To shift the energy, I asked about the substance, known as 5-MeO-DMT or the 'Rumi drug.' Intrigued by promises of experiencing nirvana, I approached with an open yet cautious mind, wanting to learn more about its potential and effects.

I asked, "Why is it called the Rumi drug?"

He answered, "Because of the profound mystical experiences it induces."

"But, why Rumi?" I asked.

"Rumi's poetry is all about divine love and union with the universe. I think you'll find that those concepts take on a different meaning after you've had this experience."

I asked what the next step would be and he said, "It would be best for us to go to the living room and create a sacred space."

We moved indoors to a dimly lit living room, setting up a ceremonial space with a large, foldable tatami sofa at its center. I took my place, feeling the spotlight of attention yet finding comfort in the setting's quiet sanctity. I could barely make out people's faces as the darkened room left little to distract from the experience ahead of me.

I was asked about my intention for the journey. Reflecting on the recent whirlwind of my 'Last Letter' book tour, I desired a ceremonial closure to that chapter of my life. It was an exhausting three months and I never really felt like it ended. One day, I just got in a plane and flew back home to Amsterdam, but there was never a sense of completion.

Jason prepared the DMT, extracted from dried toad secretion, into a potent vapor. As the room darkened further, I felt a deepening sense of safety, the ceremonial ambiance reducing distractions and heightening my focus. Lying down, I was supported physically and emotionally by friends, creating a safe container for my surrender.

There was a metal contraption equipped with a heater to melt the substance and a blower to funnel the vapor into a plastic bag. As it filled, I could see the faces of my three friends gazing at me with deep affection.

I was reclining comfortably by this time. The plastic bag swelled with the vapor, and I propped myself up slightly to inhale. My friend instructed, "Inhale deeply and hold."

Inhaling the vapor, I immediately noticed a profound silence enveloping my mind. It was like walking in from a bustling street and closing the door behind me, only to find that the room was completely soundproof—utter silence. The constant busyness of my brain was suddenly offline.

This initial sensation of tranquility was deep, and as I lay there, cradled by the presence of friends, I felt a profound sense of guidance and care.

I am familiar with the white noise that has filled my mind from a young age, having experienced its absence only during deep meditation or intense breathwork sessions. I've always found the tranquility of this state deeply soothing. Often, I've felt an underlying tension release from my body, a tension that seems rooted in the childhood trauma of living in constant fear of my father. I describe this quiet presence as "statelessness"—a sensation of being intensely present, yet simultaneously nowhere at all.

I spread out my arms and let my legs rest slightly apart, feeling the reassuring grip of friends on either side who held my hands, while my friend Sam gently placed his hands on my feet. To some, this might seem overly dramatic, but the profound love and care I felt were crucial for me to fully surrender to the experience. It felt as if this group were my guides, providing a comforting presence that eased my mind.

Shortly thereafter, another wave of sensation washed over me. It felt as if my senses were gradually shutting down, a difficult sensation to describe. It was like performing a system reboot on a computer: the machine was powered on, but none of the programs were running. My senses were present but unengaged, like instruments waiting silently for their cues.

The initial disconnection was disconcerting. Without any prior frame of reference, I struggled to comprehend the sensation, uncertain even of my own breathing as I could no longer detect air moving through my nose and mouth. However, this fleeting tension quickly dissolved as a calming voice encouraged me to let go, assuring me of safety.

Surrendering to this guidance, I encountered an experience that was nothing short of magical. A profound peace enveloped me, so complete and encompassing that it felt as though everything—absolutely everything—was perfectly alright. This tranquility deepened into a trance-like state, where my mind conjured a kaleidoscope of images on the back of my eyelids. These symmetrical shapes danced in a smooth, hypnotic pattern, drawing me further into what felt like an endless abyss.

Then, a feeling enveloped me. I experienced the profound sense of oneness often depicted in writings on enlightenment. This was not merely a philosophical idea but a deeply experienced reality. Although I was indoors, I felt an intense connection to nature in a way I never had before. The life force in the natural world became palpable, and things outside myself seemed to shift. There was a "beingness" to these objects, capturing the transformation in my perception. Before, they were mere objects; now, they revealed a profound intelligence, a presence far greater than anything I had previously comprehended, resonating on a level beyond my understanding.

There was an unexpected byproduct of this profound peace and connection: a serene acceptance of death. It felt like a return to nature, or perhaps more accurately, a return to my true nature. It was a fleeting instant where I pierced through the illusion of my constructed identity, discovering something profound beneath. It recalled a long-forgotten serenity, reminiscent of being in my mother's womb, where everything was tranquil and undisturbed. In that space, the burdens of acquired knowledge, self-image, expectations, and fears dissolved, leaving behind only the purest essence of tranquility.

As I gradually reconnected with my physical self, the profound experience did not fade. In fact, it has lingered ever since. Although not as intense, the profound connection I felt persists, much like the enduring warmth of the sun on a cool evening.

When asked about my experience, my immediate response has been that I felt the peace associated with death. I realized that my fear of death is tied to my attachment to the concept of self. When I cling to life, I fear dying. Yet, during that experience, I understood that I was already present, existing without the shackles of identity that bind us to life. As my senses functioned without attachment, I experienced a profound sense of timelessness. At that moment, I discovered a peace devoid of fear. I felt particularly connected to trees, which seemed to embody a more human-like form of existence, with branches like arms, a trunk echoing the body, and a network of roots that mirrored a brain.

This experience will be a cherished memory for the rest of my life. It was truly a gift—a rare glimpse behind the veil of an active mind into the tranquil abyss that had once been a source of profound fear for me.

That evening, my perspective on death transformed. I began to appreciate the beauty of transition. Reflecting on the night terrors of my childhood, I now perceive them with a sense of serene surrender. Previously, I could not find peace in silence, viewing it through the frightening lens of my infinite nonexistence. However, that night, I realized that my current form is part of something much grander than my individual identity. I saw the inherent beauty of the world—a world I have always been a part of and always will be. I understood that I don't need to assert my importance; I am already everything I need to be and nothing more. Now, I return to this moment, fully experiencing the essence of simply being.

MEDITATIVE QUESTIONS

Facing the Fear of the Unknown

What fears have kept you from exploring new experiences, such as minc-altering substances or other transformative practices? How can confronting these fears lead to personal growth?

Experiencing Tranquility and Statelessness

Have you ever experiencec a profound sense of peace or "statelessness"? What circumstances led to this state, and how did it impact your sense of self and the world around you?

The Concept of Oneness and Connection

Have you ever felt a deep connection to nature or a sense of oneness with the universe? What triggered this experience, and how did it change your perspective on life and death?

Finding Peace in the Present Moment

How can you cultivate a sense of peace and acceptance in your everyday life? What practices or beliefs help you stay grounded in the present moment?

CHAPTER 21

Experiencing Timelessness

As I've explored in this book, much of my journey has involved connecting to a space where death feels like a natural transition—a point where nothing ends and nothing begins, where life existed before my current awareness and continues beyond it. A significant part of this exploration has been the struggle to let go of my various identities, the personas I've believed myself to be over the years.

There's a profound melancholy I experience when I look in the mirror and realize that everything reflected back is impermanent, especially when I'm strongly identified with those reflections. Yet, there exists another state, one where the sense of impermanence shifts. In this state, looking in the mirror doesn't show a reflection of myself but something else entirely. It's less about seeing and more about experiencing—a state of being without the "me" part of it. In this mirror, I don't exist; there is only existence. In this state, the fear of dying dissipates because I am simultaneously here and not here in my present form.

This understanding is enriched by the ancient Greek concepts of time: Chronos and Kairos. Chronos refers to chronological time—time that is measured and quantifiable, like waking up at 7:00 a.m. or the sun setting at 8:35 p.m. It's quantitative and is at the root of many of the words we use to describe time today. Kairos, however, represents a different dimension of time—one that is immeasurable, without beginning or end. It's the timeless state, like standing in awe of nature's beauty, where each moment feels as if it could last forever.

The Greeks recognized that our conventional view of time was limited because it lacked a sense of timelessness. For the past decade, I have endeavored to nurture this sense of timelessness within myself. This can be challenging because it is not straightforward. It isn't about setting goals but about creating conditions that allow this state to emerge naturally. This is what I referred to in the previous chapter as a stateless experience—one that is not bound or constrained by schedules or pressures. While some people use accelerants like psychedelics to catalyze this state, my focus is on its spontaneous emergence from within, without external stimuli.

In my experience, this state often emerges when I lose attachment to parts of my identity. To understand why, consider that any thought pulling us back into concrete thinking is a return to Chronos—the linear, sequential time we seek to transcend. As Einstein suggested, problems cannot be solved within the same context in which they were created. Therefore, shifting perspective means moving beyond the confines of our established identities and habitual ways of thinking.

To touch Kairos, we must cultivate a part of our being that transcends the desire to achieve or attain a specific outcome. This part of us is unencumbered by shame or guilt, untouched by past regrets or future anxieties. For example, imagine the pure joy of a child lost in play, completely absorbed and unselfconscious, or the serenity felt during deep meditation, where time seems to stand still. In these states, moments stretch beyond the usual constraints of time, providing glimpses of a lasting presence that feels timeless and transcendent.

This concept was illustrated vividly when my friend and mentor, Cees, was diagnosed with cancer. In the initial shock, before the details were clear, he accepted his mortality and experienced a profound peace. He explained, "When I was told that I might die, I felt a comfort come over me. I immediately realized that this moment was all there was, and I felt almost electric." It was not until many years later that I realized he was touching Kairos time.

Reaching this state of Kairos doesn't require strict discipline in the conventional sense but rather a cultivation of conditions that favor its appearance. In order to nurture this space, I have learned what to avoid. This is especially true for activities that are more likely to feed my ego.

In a recent decision, I declined an invitation to a week-long sailing trip with a group of influential guests. Initially, I felt an attraction to the social prestige these individuals represented. However, as I contemplated the offer, I experienced a visceral reaction—a pulling back from the prospect. I recognized this setting as one that would distance me from my grounding state. The environment promised excitement reminiscent of an adult Disneyland: sophisticated yet fundamentally the same quick-fix allure that can distract from genuine happiness. Realizing this, I chose instead to engage in activities that support my connection to Kairos time, maintaining my commitment to a state of presence and depth, rather than fleeting thrills.

Finding the right balance between experiencing life and staying grounded is a dynamic process that each of us navigates differently throughout our lives. For me, nurturing a connection with Kairos time has enriched every day, infusing it with a special significance. I've come to understand that the essence of all life's experiences already resides within me. Seeking external experiences can often obscure this internal clarity, making it harder to perceive the profound simplicity of being. This awareness brought by Kairos time reveals that the richness of life isn't about accumulating experiences but recognizing the depth already present within ourselves.

Once the regrets of the past and the fears of tomorrow surface, we revert to Chronos time, where the anxieties of linear time prevail. Take a deep breath and envision the person you love the most. Hold on to that moment, and let it permeate every part of you. Feel it deeply. This is what it's like to be in Kairos time. Notice, though, how fragile this moment is; it can quickly disappear. The instant you worry about losing this person, or remember something you need to do, or think about what must happen next, you are thrust back into Chronos time.

To those looking to cultivate this timeless experience, I recommend practices like transcendental meditation or mindfulness. For the adventurous, psychedelics like DMT could provide a glimpse into this state, while holotropic breathwork offers a similar experience without substances.

Ultimately, nurturing this connection to timelessness allows us to experience both the peace of life and the acceptance of death, transcending identity to simply be—present and yet detached, fully immersed in the experience we call life.

MEDITATIVE QUESTIONS

Exploring Identity and Impermanence

What aspects of your identity do you find hardest to let go of? Why do you think these particular aspects are so significant to you?

Chronos and Kairos

Can you recall moments when you experienced Chronos time and Kairos time? Describe how each felt and the circumstances that led to those experiences.

Embracing Presence

Think about a time when you felt fully present and detached from worries about the past or future. What were you doing, and how did this presence affect your experience?

The Role of Environment

How does your environment influence your ability to connect with timelessness? Are there specific places or settings that help you feel more grounded and present?

CHAPTER 22

The Discipline of Facing Death

IN LIFE, SIGNIFICANT shifts often stem from one of two things: necessity or inspiration. Typically, either a situation deteriorates to the point where change becomes imperative for survival or mental well-being, or an inspiration is so powerful that it propels us towards transformation.

This also holds true when redefining our relationship with death or any profound aspect of life. As the old saying goes, insanity is doing the same thing repeatedly and expecting different results. If we desire a new perspective on death, our approach must also evolve.

In my case, it was undoubtedly a matter of necessity. As I have mentioned in previous chapters, the thought of death consumed my life. At times, it was so overwhelming that I would avoid situations where the topic might arise or steer clear of people prone to discussing it. This avoidance clearly influenced my social interactions and daily choices. Eventually, avoidance was no longer an option. I had to confront and understand my anxieties instead of allowing them to control my life. For this, discipline was required. Why? Because everything in my system would protest at the thought of addressing it. It meant doing things I would not normally do, with no guarantee of success.

This point came up one evening as I was watching the sunset over New Jersey with my friend Emily. Knowing that I had been writing this book, she turned to me with a thoughtful expression. "Andy," she began, "how do we cultivate peace with death?"

I slowed down and closed my eyes, considering her question. "That's a serious question," I replied. "I think it's similar to people who take cold baths each morning."

"Cold baths?" Emily asked, curious. "I know about them, but how does that relate to death?"

"Well," I explained, "people who take cold baths do it despite the initial discomfort because they recognize the long-term benefits. They endure the cold for the sake of improved resilience, better circulation, and overall health. It's about accepting short-term discomfort for long-term gain."

"So, by consistently facing something uncomfortable, like the concept of death, we can transform it?" Emily asked, intrigued.

"Yes, exactly," I continued. "Just as those who take cold baths eventually find a sense of well-being from their routine, we can find peace by regularly engaging with the topic of death. Initially, it's unsettling, but over time, it becomes more familiar."

Emily nodded, beginning to understand. "That makes sense. By confronting it head-on, we reduce the fear and anxiety associated with it."

"And more than that, it leads to a deeper connection to ourselves and others," I added with a smile. "Why put yourself through this if it didn't also have some benefit?"

"So, it's about finding peace in the acceptance of what we can't change," Emily said thoughtfully.

"Exactly. Just as those who take cold baths find a kind of peace in their routine discomfort, we can find peace by accepting and understanding death. It allows us to live with a sense of presence and appreciation."

"So, the key is consistency and facing the discomfort regularly?" Emily asked.

"Yes," I affirmed. "It's about making it a part of our lives, not something to be avoided. When we do that, the initial discomfort transforms into something much more manageable, even enlightening."

This approach requires us to ask key questions about our resistances. What am I resisting when I think about death? Responses vary widely: some fear nonexistence, others dread losing loved ones, and some worry about the future of those left behind. One thing is common to them all—they are uncomfortable topics to reflect upon. So why do it? This is where discipline comes in.

In my case, the fear of ceasing to exist forever was overwhelming. Facing this fear required me to actively embrace the discomfort it caused rather than avoid it. Initially, trying to sit with this fear was intensely challenging; my reactions were deep and physical.

I remember the moments well. The first few times it was hard. My blood would be pumping with night terrors and there was little chance to do much else than hear my heart beat dramatically. But in time, I began to soften the relationship with my own thoughts so that they were no longer dominating, taking me down avenues I did not want to travel.

This process turned into what I call a dance with self-awareness. Instead of reacting quickly to every thought, I learned to observe and sit with them, without judging or trying to fix them right away. It's about being present, much like listening to a partner's worries—not to solve them, but to understand and validate their feelings.

When I started this practice, my thoughts would jump quickly from one idea to another, almost like they were out of control. It felt like playing Whac-A-Mole at the arcade—I'd hit one thought down, and another would pop up right after. Learning to catch these thoughts and slow them down, while resisting the urge to solve everything right away, was the first important step.

This disciplined approach helps create a calm mind, allowing us to see life's complexities without reacting emotionally right away. By practicing this, we can reconnect with old and current emotions, letting us see our fears, like the fear of death, in a new light.

This discipline starts with personal reflection, but it's just as important to consider the impact of people, places, and experiences. The friends we choose, the places we spend our time, and the activities we engage in all play a big role in either supporting or challenging our inner peace. By paying attention to these three aspects, we can better manage our reactions and find a sense of inner balance.

For example, the people I spend time with have a significant influence on me. When I'm around individuals with deeply entrenched beliefs, I find it harder to maintain clarity. This isn't to say that having strong beliefs is inherently negative or problematic. However, if we aim to make peace with our thoughts, we must be ready to examine and possibly challenge some of our own beliefs. This process is not simple, and it may deter some from even embarking on this journey of introspection. When we live in echo chambers that are fixated on certain ways of being or seeing things, there isn't much room for alternative perspectives.

Places also have a big impact on me. For example, living in New York City means being in an intense environment. The hustle and bustle of the streets, the pollution, and the occasional squalor create a "work hard, play hard" atmosphere. This can make it challenging to find inner peace and stay connected with my deeper thoughts. While lively social events can be exciting, constantly seeking such environments can cause us to lose touch with ourselves. That's why I'm careful about choosing places that help me stay connected. For this reason, I often find sanctuary at our farm in Spain. The tranquility and nature there are a stark contrast to the urban frenzy, helping me find peace and reconnect with myself.

Experiences, especially peak ones, have given me some of my most important insights. However, actively chasing these moments can become a trap. People often seek out these experiences to cover up feelings of sadness or loneliness. The phenomenon of individuals unexpectedly committing suicide shows how these seemingly fulfilling experiences can fail to address deeper emotional voids. Continuously chasing these highs is like trying to fill a leaky bucket—the more you fill it, the more it drains, requiring even greater effort to maintain the initial high. This can create a situation where the pursuit of excitement ends up depleting our true sense of fulfillment and joy.

I vividly recall the day I confronted the profound emptiness within me. It was shortly after my mother's passing, during the conference finals at my university—a milestone I had spent my entire life preparing for. Despite being an underdog competing against markedly superior athletes, I achieved a surprisingly high placement. It should have been one of the happiest moments of my life but it was the most miserable. As I stood on the field, empty inside, I was confronted with how deeply unhappy I actually was by the mere fact that this moment could not be celebrated. That day, I walked away from track and field forever.

Maintaining discipline is seldom effortless, yet it forms a crucial foundation for cultivating inner peace and reconciling with mortality. This discipline extends to being selective about the influences we permit in our lives—the people we interact with, the places we frequent, and the experiences we pursue. While immediate gratification can be tempting, we must weigh these choices against their long-term impacts. Indulging in dessert at every meal might bring temporary pleasure, but it comes with consequences. It's vital to remain conscious of these decisions because they profoundly shape our lives and help define our "higher self"—the version of us that embodies our greatest potential.

MEDITATIVE QUESTIONS

Discipline in Practice

What practices or routines have you found helpful in building the discipline to face uncomfortable thoughts or emotions?

The Role of Environment

Consider the places you frequent. Do these environments support or hinder your ability to maintain a calm and reflective state?

The Impact of Experiences

How can you ensure that your pursuit of peak experiences aligns with your long-term well-being rather than serving as a distraction?

Understanding Higher Self

Who do you consider your "higher self" to be? How does this version of yourself approach life and death differently from your current self?

CHAPTER 23

The Practice of Doing Nothing

Preparing for death is a continual practice, evolving over time. One of the most challenging aspects I've faced is embracing the concept of doing nothing—truly nothing.

This has never been easy for me, largely due to my father's bipolar disorder. As a child, I was hypervigilant, always on edge to prevent his manic episodes. This led to a deep-seated desire to control everything, to anticipate and fix problems before they arose, making me an excellent manager but also binding me to a relentless work ethic. I often worked myself to exhaustion, ironically welcoming illness as it forced me to rest—an option I felt unable to choose under normal circumstances.

By my forties, I realized this compulsive busyness prevented me from truly feeling. This compulsion to always be active became so ingrained that I couldn't envision any alternative. I was like a hamster on a wheel, constantly running but never getting anywhere, unable to see beyond the confines of my own perpetual motion. My constant activity meant I lost the ability to simply 'be'—to be present, attuned to my thoughts, my body, and my environment without the compulsion to act.

I do not mean to suggest that one cannot both BE and do; however, mastering this balance requires practice. Consider a marksman aiming at a target. In a state of stillness and concentration, there is a high probability of success. Now, place that same marksman on the back of a moving vehicle. Suddenly, maintaining focus becomes more challenging, and greater skill is required to hit the target. This analogy underscores why I find it easier to simply BE while in nature, and why I dedicate as much time as possible each year to living on the farm.

As I already mentioned, the path to discovering inner stillness was far from direct, complicated by ingrained triggers from my turbulent relationship with my father and my reluctance to confront my own mortality. Like many others, I employed constant distractions to sidestep uncomfortable realities.

The quote from Henry David Thoreau, "The mass of men lead lives of quiet desperation," often echoed by my father, struck a chord with me; my desperation arose from a profound struggle to find tranquility in stillness.

This came up with someone I have counseled for years. One day, I sat in Ray's office, discussing his struggles with the concept of doing nothing. "Why is it so hard for me to do nothing?" He asked, a hint of frustration in his voice.

I smiled, understanding his dilemma. "Because doing nothing feels like losing control," I replied. "It's about trusting that the world will keep spinning without your constant input. It's about accepting that you're not the one holding everything together."

"I get that in theory," Ray said, stirring his tea thoughtfully. "But every time I try to sit still, I feel this anxiety, like I'm wasting time or missing out on something important."

I nodded in empathy. "It's a practice, not a quick fix," I reassured him. "You've spent years in a state of constant vigilance, especially in your work environment. Your brain is wired to always be on high alert. Changing that wiring takes time and patience. It's about learning to observe your thoughts without getting attached to them, like watching clouds passing in the sky."

Learning to observe my thoughts without attachment marked a significant shift. I mention this often throughout this book because it was a pivotal moment for me, and I believe it can be transformative for anyone looking to change their way of being. This practice wasn't about solving or escaping my thoughts but about giving them space. This shift didn't eliminate my challenges, but it allowed me to engage with them differently, experiencing life with newfound freedom.

My practice isn't about sitting in a yoga pose each morning, but rather catching the moments when I experience a shift in my consciousness. A judgment towards someone, a feeling of anger, a wave of sadness—anything that suddenly appears, like a new blip on a submarine radar. This approach helps me maintain a peaceful mind, which is crucial for managing the busyness that once dominated my life.

Despite understanding the value of inactivity, I still experience moments of escapism, such as binge-watching dramas on Netflix, which ironically aren't truly relaxing. However, I've learned not to judge these phases harshly, recognizing them as part of my journey toward finding balance.

In essence, doing nothing is about allowing life to unfold without forcing action or reaction. It's about learning to be present with whatever arises, finding peace in the stillness that once felt so threatening. This is how I prepare for death—not as an end but as a profound part of life, embracing the quiet that ultimately brings the deepest peace.

MEDITATIVE QUESTIONS

Embracing Stillness

Reflect on a time when you allowed yourself to do nothing. What emotions or thoughts surfaced during this period?

Hypervigilance and Control

Consider the role of control in your life. How does the need to control your environment and outcomes impact your ability to find stillness?

Mindful Escapism

Reflect on your habits of escapism, such as binge-watching TV shows. How do these habits affect your sense of stillness and peace?

Preparing for Transitions

How does the practice of doing nothing prepare you for life's inevitable transitions, including death?

CHAPTER 24

Getting Comfortable with Silence

IF DOING NOTHING was the beginning of making peace, then embracing silence is the next step. Cue Simon and Garfunkel's "The Sound of Silence" echoing in my mind: "Hello darkness, my old friend. I've come to talk with you again." It's like they're serenading my journey into the abyss of tranquility.

Beneath the busyness that carried me through much of my life, I have always harbored a fear of silence. Sitting with silence was challenging for me throughout my childhood and much of my adulthood. This inability to embrace silence made it hard for me to fall asleep, as my mind would race with thoughts in the quiet, amplifying my discomfort. As a child, I even resorted to bumping my head against my pillow to fall asleep, as it was the only way I could silence the thoughts.

This was clearly not sustainable and led to health problems throughout my thirties. Part of this overactive mind certainly had a touch of ADHD, but there was also an underlying fear—the fear of silence. To me, silence felt like the closest thing to death without actually being dead. Falling asleep was fraught with anxiety, seen through the lens that one day I'd close my eyes for good. Who's to say that this won't be the last time?

As my health issues were arising, I realized that I needed to make some changes. Although I did not formally join a mindfulness or a meditation course, I began to slow down and hear my thoughts, as I mentioned in the previous chapters. I slowed down my thinking to the point that the voice inside my head was getting easier to hear.

In the quiet stillness, the concept of mortality crept into my consciousness. But this time, I did not turn to busyness to distract from it. And then something changed. With this newfound quiet, I was now face to face with the fear I'd spent my life avoiding. This shadow had always been there, like a monster under the bed, fueling my imagination. For the first time, I was looking directly at it. No more hiding.

Instead of asking myself difficult questions that made my mind race with fear, I started asking gentler, more caring ones. Questions like, "What do you feel when these thoughts come up?" helped me explore my emotions with more compassion. I also asked, "How has avoiding these thoughts been affecting you?" which made me see how avoiding them was changing my life in small but important ways. Lastly, I wondered, "Why don't you feel safe asking for help?" This question helped me understand my vulnerabilities and the barriers I had built against seeking support.

This issue arose with a dear friend whom I had supported through the years, as they struggled to sit with silence.

"Andy, have you ever found it hard to just sit in silence?" he asked.

I looked at him thoughtfully before responding. "Silence used to terrify me. It's when all my fears and doubts came to the surface."

He nodded, relieved to hear he wasn't alone. "Yeah, I know. For me, it's always been uncomfortable. I don't know what is going to show up in the quiet."

I leaned back in my chair, reflecting. "When I first started to slow down my thinking, it was excruciating, sitting there with my thoughts. But gradually, I began to see it differently. Silence became a space where I could actually hear myself think, without the noise of the world drowning me out."

My words resonated deeply with him. "I do see fears come up," he shared. "Like, 'What will I change in my life?' I see that there are certain answers that I am not yet willing to confront."

I smiled. "I understand. Once you start asking questions, you open yourself up to the fact that there are some answers you might not like."

"Most certainly," he said. "And yet, I don't really feel like I have much of a choice."

I nodded. "Silence can be a mirror. It reflects our deepest fears but also our true selves. It's not easy, but it was a hurdle I needed to cross to find peace in my head."

This conversation, or variations of it, frequently arises with the people I interact with, especially those who keep themselves so busy that they are unable to hear their own thoughts.

With this silence began a new relationship with myself. It was not easy at first. I started to discover a wealth of insights that were hanging around in the cellar of my mind. I realized I had a deep fear of not being enough, a constant need for validation from others, and an untapped depth of creativity. This newfound understanding helped me better grasp the fears and emotions of others. In the silence, I could explore the many conflicting emotions within me.

I realized that I did not want to die; I desperately wanted to exist, and the thought of my existence being wiped away was utterly incapacitating. I also uncovered buried fears, like the fear of failing those I care about or of never truly being understood. I found a deep-seated need for acceptance and a capacity for compassion that I had often ignored.

When I sat with that fear and embraced the silence, something special began to emerge. This journey started with my relationship with silence and has evolved throughout my life, continually bringing me back to the concept of identity. By embracing the quiet, I learned to navigate the complexities within me, gaining a clearer understanding of who I am and what truly matters.

When I think about death, I go back to the mirror that I mentioned previously. I think about the loss of the person whom I refer to as "Andy." It may sound obvious to say, "I am Andy." When I look in a mirror, he is reflected back to me. Isn't it obvious? And yet, in the silence, there was a deeper exploration behind that idea.

I began to see that Andy was also a creation in my head. I'd spent a great deal of my life forming an identity around who Andy was and what was important for him. How he wanted to be viewed by others and what he wanted to achieve in his life. It was in and through silence that these thoughts became less stiff and more pliable.

Letting go of my self-imposed identities was so jarring that I nearly lost all sense of reality when confronted by my mentor, Cees. As he "called me out" on all of my delusional behavior, I felt the foundation of who I believed myself to be crumbling. I remember sweating in bed for three days straight, the first time I truly grasped this concept. My entire world seemed to collapse around me. Yet, I needed to confront this in my own life to make peace with death. The fear of death looms large only when I believe that my identity is dying—the very idea of who I am. When that idea is no longer dominant, death becomes less frightening, allowing me to be present without attachment to my identity.

It is in that silence that I have embarked on my own practice of preparing to die—by fully living. I qualify the word "fully" with the caveat that I strive to navigate life with a profound inclination towards introspection. This is not about judging myself or feeling that I should be better, but about cultivating a genuine connection to the experience of being alive. I have found that time spent with others either invigorates me or depletes me; there is rarely any middle ground in my life.

I gain energy from people when we are truly engaged in a dialogue. I use the word "dialogue" to describe a space where two people listen to and understand each other, genuinely wanting to connect, not just waiting for their turn to speak. This is different from what I call transactional communication, which I do my best to avoid. I often find that people who are waiting to speak are not spending much time listening. It is the silence that allows for magical moments to emerge. It is like the moment I shared with my Japanese friend Hideki, crying at the table without a word needing to be spoken. This silence is achievable only when all the identities within me, which have been fighting to be heard, are no longer active. This doesn't mean they are gone; they simply no longer unconsciously drive my behavior.

If you have not yet built a relationship with silence, I encourage you to find ways to do so. This can be done either though mindfulness practices or even joining a silent retreat. Silence has brought me more power than the use of words. And in that quiet, which has come over years of letting go of who I thought I was, I've evolved to become a more loving and compassionate person. That development was attached to my fear of death. Until I was able to make peace with my nonexistence, I was not able to fully embrace living. And it all starts with silence.

MEDITATIVE QUESTIONS

Facing Inner Thoughts

When you sit in silence, what kinds of thoughts typically surface? How do you usually respond to these thoughts?

Overcoming Busyness

What role does busyness play in your life? How does constant activity impact your ability to find inner peace?

Dialogue and Connection

How does silence impact your ability to engage in meaningful dialogue with others? How can you cultivate more spaces for genuine connection in your interactions?

Preparing for Death

How does silence help you confront your fears of death and nonexistence? What insights have you gained from sitting with these fears in silence?

CHAPTER 25

The Gift of Surrender

LET'S FACE IT, although people may be living in deep discomfort, the decision to stay with the familiar often outweighs the fear of change. But why? Why do we cling to something that doesn't serve us? Consider those who remain in unfulfilling jobs for the security of a steady income, or those who stay in toxic relationships because starting over feels more intimidating. We are creatures of habit, even when those habits aren't serving us.

Sometimes, I feel like my primary role in life is to hold space for people until they decide to break free from patterns that no longer serve them. It's like the often-used metaphor of a caterpillar transforming into a butterfly. This special moment of transformation has many names: finding one's authentic self, embracing inner freedom, achieving true alignment, discovering genuine purpose, or stepping into one's full potential. Choose the one that resonates best with you.

The interesting thing about this is that, more often than not, asking a person who their "authentic self" is will be met with a blank face. After one has contorted themselves for so many years to adapt to society and their surroundings, it's difficult to distinguish who one truly is and who they have become to survive. Yes, there may be a general sense, but clarity is often elusive. Supporting people through this process of transformation is not always easy, as it takes patience. There is an aspect to this change which requires a leap of faith, a moment of surrender with no guarantees of success.

I experienced this tension when my mentor Cees died. He was not only a dear friend but also my business partner. We had worked together for a decade, and after his passing, everything we had built no longer made sense to me. I was left asking myself, "What am I going to do now?" I found myself trapped in loops of unanswerable questions. Fears arose, and excuses emerged about why certain things were not possible, even before I had begun. Amidst this chaos, I made a simple decision: to write my first book. I didn't know what I would write about or where to start, but I surrendered to the thought, "I have no idea what to do with my life, and this feels right."

This confused many people around me, who made typical comments like, "What makes you think you can write a book?" and "Do you really have anything that interesting to say?" But I didn't listen to these voices because I had already surrendered to a process with no clear outcome in sight. I only knew that I would write a book, and I trusted that it would guide me. As you can see, it has.

What I learned through this experience, and have had to nurture in myself over the years, is that the answers often don't come until the end. Since the outcome is unknowable ahead of time, I must follow a deeper sense of intuition. This isn't easy because it requires surrendering to an uncertain future.

This all brings me to the story of a dear friend, David, whom I've occasionally mentored. Just prior to his 32nd birthday, David consumed psychedelic mushrooms, as he had done several times before, without considering his surroundings—his apartment on the fourth floor. During the peak of his experience, he found himself pondering profound questions at his window: How do I transform my life? How do I align to my authentic self? How do I escape this relentless cycle of frustration?

As he looked out, he considered surrendering to a force greater than himself, to the idea that fate will unfold as intended. Compelled by this thought, he stepped out the window. Miraculously, a taxi cushioned his fall. He survived, albeit with several broken bones and narrowly escaping death.

When I asked him about his reasons for jumping, he explained, "At that moment, I was driven by anger towards the part of me that was fearful. I felt an intense urge to rid myself of it. It was like an inner, rebellious child wanting to assert himself—to prove his existence beyond just this physical form."

"What pushed you to take that final step?" I inquired further.

After a thoughtful pause, he responded, "It was trust. I was reaching out to the deepest, most buried part of myself, hidden beneath layers of fear and pain."

"As I stood at that window, despite my body trembling with the fear of death, I trusted the same guidance that had led me to this point in life would see me through if I took the leap. And it did. My life has since unfolded with a deeper magic. I surrendered to the destiny life had prepared for me."

Although many people in our shared circle of friends judged him for his actions, I felt a strange admiration. It is not easy to write this, as I can imagine those same people labeling me as crazy. But I view this story through a different lens. I sit in awe of the profound level of surrender and the transformative journey that followed. I've always believed that allowing things to unfold requires deep surrender, much like a base jumper stepping off a cliff and trusting that the parachute will open, even if they can't ever be entirely sure.

David took the leap, quite literally, fully embracing the uncertainty that came with it. While I certainly do not want to romanticize his actions and risk encouraging others to follow suit, I deeply appreciate his remarkable level of surrender. His willingness to face the unknown without a safety net is both extraordinary and courageous.

Since childhood, surrendering to the flow of life has been

challenging for me, fraught with fear and anxiety stemming from my father's unpredictable rages and the everyday difficulties life brings. Like many, I crave control. However, life does not grant us that. Instead, it presents us with unpredictable, life-changing moments. Some people experience this more intensely than others.

Throughout this book, I've referred to these transitions as "little deaths." They involve the loss of something significant—be it a past era, a childhood home, or a cherished relationship. Yet, there's another dimension to this concept. How we frame a situation often determines how we experience it. As Anaïs Nin famously said, "We don't see things as they are, we see them as we are." This idea is echoed in the parable of "The Farmer and the Horse," where each potentially negative event is met with the response, "Maybe. We'll see."

I would like to take a moment to highlight this counterpoint. We have the choice to simultaneously mourn the loss of something while, at the same time, surrendering to an uncertain future. I liken this to pruning a tree to inspire new growth. Just as the tree thrives after being pruned, we too can flourish by letting go and allowing new possibilities to emerge.

David's decision can be viewed through two lenses: either he jumped to end his life or to embrace a new one. Had he died and his story remained untold, we might have all considered it a suicide. Fortunately, he survived, offering us a story to reflect on in relationship to our own surrender.

This example is extreme, and I do not condone such drastic actions. However, David's intent wasn't to end his life but to embrace a new form of existence—a leap into the unknown, beyond his current comprehension. His courageous act invites us to contemplate our own capacity for surrender and transformation.

When I think about death, I often reflect on David's bravery in diving into the unknown, trusting that whatever comes next will be different but manageable. This idea can be terrifying—the fear of losing everything forever. But when I view life through the lens of permanent loss or surrendering to an uncertain future, my perspective changes profoundly. On one hand, there's the weight of the loss; on the other, there are new possibilities that we can only understand in hindsight.

It's a strange paradox: letting go of the fear of death to truly feel alive. My fear of death often felt like it was holding me back, making me feel like I wasn't really living.

This reminds me of the days when I struggle to accept what's happening around me. Ideally, I would embrace everything that comes my way and go with the flow. However, when I resist my feelings, including the fear of death, they can take over and consume me.

As you navigate your own path, I encourage you to explore where you feel constrained and to apply the practice of self-compassion I discuss in my books: acknowledge your deepest fears, and follow them with, "and that's okay."

For instance, "I am afraid to die, and that's okay." "I am overwhelmed by the fear of the unknown, and that's okay."

By embracing surrender, we unlock the door to future possibilities. We opt to embrace the opportunities that come our way, rather than dwelling on what we've left behind. This mindset shift has reshaped my existence, transitioning it from one characterized by pain to one filled with acceptance, presence, and flow.

MEDITATIVE QUESTIONS

Fear of Change

Reflect on a time when you clung to something familiar despite knowing it wasn't serving you. What held you back from making a change?

Letting Go

What are you currently holding on to that no longer serves you? How can you begin the process of letting go?

Framing Experiences

How does your perspective influence your experience of events in your life? Can you think of a situation where changing your perspective helped you cope better?

Self-Compassion

Reflect on the practice of self-compassion

"I am afraid to die, and that's okay." How can this mindset help you navigate your fears and anxieties?

CHAPTER 26

Moments of Reflection

DEATH WHISPERS TO me at 37,000 feet. Amidst the hum of jet engines and the soft glow of cabin lights, I find myself confronting life's impermanence in the most unexpected of places—hurtling through the sky. Long-haul flights, especially over vast oceans, have become my airborne sanctuaries for reflection. Here, with minimal distractions and the stark separation from my loved ones, I am acutely aware of the thin veil between life and death. The altitude amplifies my introspection, turning each journey into a profound meditation on mortality.

A survey by Virgin Atlantic revealed that I am not alone in experiencing heightened emotions during flights. The survey found that a significant number of people report increased emotional sensitivity while flying. Specifically, 41% of men admitted to hiding their tears under a blanket, and 55% of all respondents said that flying intensified their emotions.[3] This phenomenon, often referred to as "weepy warnings," prompted the airline to issue alerts before showing particularly sad movies on their flights.

---

3 Source: https://www.theguardian.com/film/2011/aug/18/virgin-atlantic-films-warning

I've found that this environment strips away many of the distractions that clutter my daily life. It's here, in this suspended reality, that I confront the fragility of life most starkly. Every bump of turbulence serves as a stark reminder that I am not in control. It highlights the profound reality of our existence: our time is finite, and each moment is precious.

During these flights, I often find myself writing letters to the people I cherish. There's something magical about this high-altitude perspective—it offers a rare opportunity to express the significant impact others have had on my life. It nudges me toward a deep surrender. It compels me to consider: If this were my last moment, what would I want to say, and to whom?

The power of such moments is so profound that it compels me to take actions that might otherwise seem unnecessary or premature. It was this intensity that drove me to write a letter to my mother when it didn't seem urgent, to take my friend Cees on a trip even though we thought we had years before his passing, and to spontaneously embark on the Last Letter tour, which I detail throughout this book. These experiences highlight a compelling force that, when embraced, pushes me to act decisively. This drive fills my life and interactions with deep meaning, urging me to seize moments that might otherwise be delayed.

I understand that these moments can be confrontational, challenging us to confront the weight of our own existence. Yet, they also offer solace, revealing that life, with all its complexity and unpredictability, can hold profound meaning at any moment we choose.

Think of someone who holds special significance in your life—perhaps someone who supported you in your childhood or did you a favor more recently. Now, take 20 minutes to write them a letter or an email. Write as if you had just learned they had only a few weeks to live. Pour your heart into expressing your gratitude, affection, and any unspoken sentiments. Then, send it. You have just created a meaningful moment for both you and that person.

Navigating this mindset is delicate, balancing on the fine line between accepting the potential for pain and embracing the energy to act. Some might question the value of such reflections, arguing that they lead to depression. However, as I mentioned in the previous chapter, how we frame a situation defines how we experience it. For instance, the thought "I'm going to die, that's terrible" frames death in helplessness. Conversely, "I'm going to die. Wouldn't it be beautiful to share with people what they mean to me?" frames it in a potentially transformative light. This reframing allows us to find beauty and meaning even in the face of life's most challenging realities.

Death, therefore, serves not only as a reminder of our mortality but also as a muse, inspiring us to live with urgency and intention. The unique conditions of air travel provide a quiet space to contemplate our helplessness and vulnerability, yet, also to forge deep connections and articulate unsaid feelings.

When I land and step back into the rush of life, I carry with me a renewed sense of purpose and a deeper commitment to live intentionally. Each flight, each journey above the clouds, serves as a poignant reminder: life is fleeting, and each moment is an opportunity to craft the story we wish to leave behind.

MEDITATIVE QUESTIONS

Confronting Life's Fragility

How do you typically respond to situations that remind you of life's fragility? Do these moments prompt any specific actions or reflections?

Writing Letters

Have you ever written a letter to someone as a way to express your feelings? What impact did it have on your relationship with that person?

Taking Decisive Actions

Reflect on a time when you took a decisive action, prompted by a sense of urgency. What motivated you to act, and what was the outcome?

Sharing Unspoken Feelings

Is there someone in your life to whom you haven't fully expressed your gratitude or affection? What's holding you back from doing so?

Seeing Through the Matrix

As WE WANDERED through the labyrinthine streets of old Amsterdam, my friend suddenly stopped and looked at me with a puzzled expression. "How do you stay so calm and collected?" he blurted out, catching me off guard. "What's your secret to not folding under life's struggles?"

Pausing by a canal, I gestured to the surroundings and began, "Nothing you see here today existed 400 years ago. It has all been created. Even the very street beneath our feet was once a swamp, unrecognizable from its current form. This is a constructed reality. It all feels so real that we call it reality. And these are just the things we can see and touch. Beyond these physical structures lie invisible forces—societal norms, cultural expectations, religious beliefs, and educational influences—that have been shaping us for centuries."

My friend nodded, intrigued. "What do you mean? How does this create calm?"

"We lose that calm when deeply held beliefs are so ingrained that we accept them as undeniable truths, often reinforcing societal norms through our judgments," I replied with a smile. "Although I live within this constructed reality, I'm also aware that it's artificial.

Life feels like being on a theater stage, with each day offering a chance to interact with the set pieces of this grand play."

"But doesn't that desensitize you to life? Doesn't it make life seem… less real?" my friend asked, a bit perplexed.

"I found it to be quite the opposite. Recognizing our reality as a construct can be deeply grounding," I continued. "It allows me to shape my own personal reality. Society sets the basic rules, defining what's acceptable or not, and these standards change over time. Just think about how societal views on alcohol in the 1920s or same-sex marriage a decade ago have transformed. By understanding that these norms are fluid, I can take control and redefine my reality."

"I like that perspective," my friend said thoughtfully. "But how do you deal with the idea that everything we believe is just a construct? Isn't that overwhelming?"

"It can be," I admitted. "For some, this realization is really overwhelming, leading to existential crises, substance abuse, or a descent into nihilism. It's an intimidating realization, much like Neo's in *The Matrix*, where everything you've valued and believed in is revealed as an illusion, fundamentally changing your life and worldview. This new perspective makes you question everything, taking away the comfort of your illusions and forcing you to face the raw reality of existence."

"That sounds intense," my friend remarked. "How do you cope with it?"

"This awareness peels back the layers of societal conditioning within us," I explained. "Why do we feel such strong emotions during national anthems? Why do we seek validation through likes on social media? Even our ideas of success and happiness are shaped by societal expectations. Letting go of these ingrained behaviors allows us to truly shape our lives according to our deepest desires, not what society expects of us."

"This sounds liberating, but I still wonder how this translates into calm?" my friend asks thoughtfully.

"Yes, calm." I acknowledged. "With this insight, your options in life expand. You could follow many different paths. Maybe one falls into addiction, or shines in business, or travels the world in a van. The point is that freedom comes from living your own life on your own terms. Understanding this gives you the opportunity to shape your life without needing society's approval, freeing yourself from its constraints. And that is, as far as I am concerned, very calming."

"But how do you balance that with living in a society that clings to these constructs?" my friend asked.

"Navigating this balance is a daily responsibility," I responded. "I respect and engage with the shared reality while being aware that it's constructed. I consider societal judgments to connect with others, but I don't let them control me. I try to live with dual perspectives: respecting our shared reality but also seeing beyond societal fabrications."

"That's a delicate balance," my friend acknowledged.

"The bigger question for me is, how do I create the reality I want?" I continued. "I see this through the concept of vision—living as if the reality I desire already exists. My mentor once said, 'A vision is a reality lived ahead of its completion.' Start living today as you imagine your future self. At first, you might face skepticism, but over time, those who doubted will see and admire your achievements. Just like the people who laughed at me when I started writing books."

"So, you're saying we should live as if we're already the person we aspire to be?" my friend asked, beginning to grasp the concept.

"That's it," I confirmed. "In short, nothing should stop you from going after what you want in the time you have left. Even though society might tell you otherwise, living within the "Matrix" isn't mandatory. As Mary Oliver asks in her famous poem, "Tell me, what is it you plan to do with your one wild and precious life?" This isn't just a poetic question—it's a call to action, inviting us to live authentically and fully, beyond the limits of constructed realities."

My friend smiled, inspired by our conversation. "Thank you. This has given me a lot to think about."

As C.G. Jung famously said, "The privilege of a lifetime is to become who you truly are." This profound statement serves as a guiding light in our journey through life, inviting us to defy skepticism, transcend societal limits, and realize our true potential.

Throughout our lives, we are often surrounded by constructs—societal norms, cultural expectations, and personal beliefs—that shape our reality. These constructs can feel so real that we accept them as absolute truths. Yet, recognizing them as fluid and changeable allows us to reclaim our personal power and reshape our lives according to our deepest desires.

MEDITATIVE QUESTIONS

The Balance Between Awareness and Engagement

How do you navigate the balance between engaging with societal norms and maintaining your awareness of their constructed nature?

Expanding Personal Reality

Think about an area of your life where you feel constrained by societal expectations. How might you redefine this area to better align with your true desires?

Overcoming Societal Judgments

How do societal judgments impact your decisions and actions? How can you minimize their influence on your life?

The Power of Vision

How does the concept of living as if your desired reality already exists resonate with you? How can this mindset shift your approach to achieving your goals?

CHAPTER 28

Achieving Balance

IF YOU WERE to ask me, "Andy, what are you seeking in life?" I would answer, without hesitation, "balance." I respond so swiftly because I've seen the chaos that ensues when my life falls out of balance—days lose their meaning, distractions multiply, and I become disconnected from both myself and others.

One story that deeply resonates with me is the tale of Siddhartha Gautama, known as the Buddha. One day, while meditating under the Bodhi tree, he had a moment of deep insight. He realized that neither extreme indulgence nor extreme austerity led to enlightenment. Instead, he discovered the Middle Way, a path of moderation and balance. This understanding brought him enlightenment and laid the foundation for Buddhism.

The key idea is about keeping things simple and balanced. Enlightenment doesn't come from extreme practices but from realizing that extremes are unnecessary. This makes me think of the saying, "It's not about the destination, it's about the journey."

During a visit to a lakeside retreat, I reconnected with an old friend, Thay, whom I had met years before at a conference. A Buddhist monk, he radiated a calm that matched the peaceful surroundings.

"Andy, what are you seeking in life?" he asked as we sat on the dock.

"A balanced life," I replied, feeling the weight of the word. "I've seen my life fall apart when I lose it."

Thay nodded. "What brought you to this realization?"

"I used to think I needed big changes to fix my life—new courses, big decisions, jumping into relationships. But after years of swinging between extremes, I realized the problem wasn't external. It was my way of being."

"Ah, the Middle Way," Thay said. "Extremes are tempting, but they rarely lead to peace."

"I've chased experiences, hoping they'd give my life meaning, but they often left me feeling empty," I admitted.

"Attachment to experiences can be a trap," he said. "We mistake the thrill for fulfillment."

I nodded, thinking of my adventures. "I was running from myself."

Thay smiled. "True peace comes from within, not from external adventures."

"It hasn't been easy," I said. "But slowing down and facing my fears has brought me deeper tranquility."

"The quiet within us is powerful," he said. "It's where we find our true selves."

"But balance isn't easy," I pointed out. "Too much introspection can lead to confusion and loneliness."

"Yes," Thay agreed. "Balance is a dynamic journey. It's about navigating extremes with mindfulness."

"That's what I'm striving for," I said. "To understand myself, maintain balance, and stay connected to others."

"It's a noble path," he said, placing a hand on my shoulder. "Remember, balance takes time and practice. Be kind to yourself along the way."

This journey towards equilibrium is deeply entwined with my reflections on mortality, resonating with the Buddhist tenet of non-attachment. Buddhism teaches that attachment inevitably brings about suffering; therefore, even an attachment to life itself can be a source of anguish. However, this should not be misconstrued as an encouragement for a bleak resignation from life or an adoption of a nihilistic belief that everything is inconsequential.

Balance is key here. I enjoy life's joys, but I balance them with moments of quiet reflection. My life gets out of balance when I start chasing experiences, hoping they'll give my life meaning. At first, these pursuits are fulfilling, but they soon fail to hide the underlying sadness that everything will eventually end. Before understanding this, my life was a constant effort to seek ever more intense experiences, trying to surpass each previous high.

A recent experience highlighted this cycle for me. I attended a high school basketball game where the energy was electric. Caught up in the excitement, I cheered until I lost my voice. Although the victory was exhilarating, I soon felt a familiar emotional crash—a feeling that haunted my twenties and thirties as I sought peak experiences to fill the existential void I associated with death. This cycle of highs and lows reminded me that seeking extreme moments often led to emptiness, not fulfillment.

Travel also filled this gap for me. Driven by a desire to be seen as a worldly adventurer and a deep need to get the high from another cultural experience, I found it difficult to maintain long-term relationships. How could I, when I was always running from my emotions and moving on to the next destination? Only by slowing down and facing my fears did I begin to find a deeper peace and a different kind of beauty in life—not from external adventures but from a profound internal tranquility.

When my life was full of existential questions that led to more unanswerable questions, I found myself lost and confused. It's important not to confuse introspection with overthinking. People often fall into two camps: those who think they can outthink their feelings, trying to analyze emotions into something manageable, and those who get so absorbed in thought that they miss living life.

After my mother's death, I emotionally shut down and became isolated. The journey to inner peace isn't about avoiding emotions or seeking definitive answers; it's about experiencing and balancing the extremes. Sometimes, what I needed was a good cry, not another conversation about how sad I was. Finding a dynamic midpoint that continually shifts is the essence of the Middle Way.

The "how" to find balance does not have a straightforward answer. In previous chapters, I discussed avoiding situations, places, and people that tend to disrupt my balance. But there's more to it. When I'm out of balance, I can feel it, but I don't always know what to do about it.

Yesterday, I called a friend who had been struggling with cancer for years. I knew he was having a hard time, but I didn't realize how severe it was. It was a video call from his partner, using his account. I expected to see him, but she answered the call with a solemn face and shared that he had, in her words, "transitioned yesterday." She then turned the phone to show him, and in a matter of seconds, I was looking at the lifeless body of a dear friend. I felt completely out of balance. I wanted to cry, yet the tears were hidden beneath the confusion of this unexpected moment. I gazed at him for about a minute and said, "I love you, brother. I'm gonna miss you."

I spent the next day feeling out of balance, sitting with feelings of disconnection from my deeper emotions: pain, helplessness, grief. The pain was just beneath the surface, unable to fully emerge. So, what did I do? I slowed down. I allowed myself to feel and eventually wept. What I didn't do was occupy myself with distractions, which is what I—and many others—tend to do when strong emotions arise. In my life, finding balance has been more about recognizing when I am out of balance and slowing down to let my system untangle itself.

At the core, it's about slowing down at critical moments. It's about understanding your inclinations and aversions—what draws you in, what pushes you away, and how these preferences shape your life. Leaving metaphorical breadcrumbs in your mind helps you find your way back to emotional connection. This practice may require effort, but the consequences of neglecting it are profound and real.

MEDITATIVE QUESTIONS

Seeking Balance

Think about a time when your life felt out of balance. What were the consequences, and how did you regain equilibrium?

Balancing Joy and Reflection

Think of a recent experience where you sought joy externally. What did you learn from this experience about your own needs for balance?

Introspection vs. Overthinking

Reflect on the difference between healthy introspection and overthinking. How do you ensure that your introspective practices are beneficial rather than overwhelming?

Understanding Preferences and Aversions

What are your main inclinations and aversions? How do they impact your ability to achieve balance in your life?

CHAPTER 29

Expectations, Forgiveness and Death

THERE CAME A time in my life when I stopped blaming others for my feelings. Instead of saying, "You made me feel this way," I began to express, "I feel this way when I interact with you." This might seem like a subtle distinction, but it profoundly changes how one interacts with the world. In the former, the other is seen as the problem; in the latter, the issue lies within me. Yes, the other may be the trigger, but I hold responsibility for my reactions.

This realization centers around the expectations we set for others, ourselves, society, and how we anticipate things will unfold in our lives. Often, it's these unspoken expectations—the ones we aren't even conscious of—that cause us the deepest pain. These include societal scripts about life's milestones, such as when to marry, how friendships should evolve, when to achieve career success, the type of lifestyle we should maintain, how we should parent, when to buy a house, and what retirement should look like. These unacknowledged expectations can be the source of deep anguish.

Recently, a friend called me, devastated by a divorce. He had married young, full of dreams about a future filled with shared experiences, mutual support, and unwavering love. He envisioned growing old together, watching their children flourish, and celebrating life's milestones hand in hand. But reality had dealt him a different hand. The relationship had deteriorated over the years, eroded by misunderstandings, unmet expectations, and growing emotional distance.

As he poured out his heart, I listened attentively, knowing that sometimes the best support comes from simply being there, offering a compassionate ear. He spoke of the nights spent arguing, the moments of silence that spoke louder than words, and the gradual realization that the person he had married was no longer the same.

"This isn't what I envisioned," he said again, the pain evident in his voice. "We were supposed to grow old together. We had plans, dreams…"

I could hear the anguish and confusion in his voice. It wasn't just the end of a marriage he was mourning; it was the death of a dream, the loss of a future he had so meticulously crafted in his mind. He was grappling with the profound disappointment of reality not aligning with his expectations, and it was tearing him apart.

At that moment, I realized that his struggle was not just about the relationship, but about reconciling the gap between his dreams and his reality. The divorce had forced him to confront the disparity between what he had hoped for and what life had actually given him.

"You know," I said gently, "sometimes the hardest part is letting go of the life we envisioned. It's okay to mourn that loss. But remember, it's also an opportunity to create a new vision, a new future, one that might be different but can still be fulfilling."

My friend was mourning the "little death" of unmet expectations—actually, several of them. These losses are often confusing and complex, filled with ambiguous grief that's difficult to unravel. These type of "little deaths" account for over 90 percent of the challenges in the people I coach.

People often "spin" by retelling the same story repeatedly

because they can't find internal resolution. Signs of spinning include rehashing conflicts without making progress, struggling to move past losses, or holding on to relationships that have long ended. When faced with life's upheavals, these hidden hopes and unresolved issues surface, revealing the depth of our unacknowledged desires.

A friend, Maria, sat across from me, her frustration palpable. "I wanted him to always be there for me, to understand my needs without me having to spell them out," she said, a hint of indignation in her voice. "I mean, isn't that what love is supposed to be?"

"Love can indeed involve deep understanding," I agreed, "but expecting someone to always know what you need without communication is a heavy burden. It's an assumption that can lead to disappointment and frustration."

"But shouldn't he just know?" she insisted. "We were together for years!"

I nodded, understanding her pain. "It's natural to hope for that kind of connection. However, when those unspoken desires aren't met, it can cause a lot of distress. It's important to communicate your needs clearly."

She sighed, a mix of exasperation and sadness. "I just thought if he loved me enough, he would know."

"This brings us to an important point," I said gently. "Unspoken desires often go unrecognized until they cause problems. You wanted him to understand you completely without needing to express yourself. When he didn't, it felt like a betrayal, but it was more about the assumption than his actual behavior."

She looked down, processing my words. "So, you're saying it's my fault for expecting too much?"

"It's not about fault," I clarified. "It's about recognizing those assumptions and understanding their impact. It's also about realizing that everyone has limitations and can't meet unspoken needs all the time."

Her eyes softened. "I see. I guess I never thought about it that way. I always assumed that if the love was real, everything would just... fall into place."

Although most of us don't want to admit it, we are very much like Maria. We hold on to idealized images of how things should be, which leads to pain when reality doesn't match up. I've experienced this dynamic in my relationship with my father. From early on, we were often at odds. No matter how hard I tried to please him, he always found fault and wanted me to be someone different. This led to deep discord throughout our lives.

From my earliest memories, my father and I clashed constantly. He was always criticizing me, and every time I didn't meet his expectations, it led to explosive arguments. The breaking point came when I returned early from a year-long backpacking trip, only to tell him I was leaving again soon. He was perpetually frustrated, accusing me of not taking my life seriously and "running away from my responsibilities." He never missed an opportunity to remind me of this in our conversations. He had expected me to settle down in the US, so when I shared my plans to leave again, his anger boiled over, and he threw me out of the house. We didn't speak for the next ten years.

This highlights a common theme: when our expectations aren't met, it often leads to significant emotional fallout.

My father fixated on justifying his actions, spinning the same stories over and over again. He was trapped in the same blindness that many people face, unable to see that our impulsive reactions are driven by our own unmet expectations, not by others' actions.

On the other hand, I spent years holding on to resentment, focusing on my father's faults and spinning my own stories about how horrible he was. It wasn't until a mentor urged me to consider his motivations that I realized his actions were driven by fear and love, not malice. This realization was profound and difficult to articulate. Even now, it feels like words don't fully capture the depth of that understanding.

I realized that my expectations of what a father "should be" had clouded my ability to see him as a person, not just as a father. I had to process a "little death"—the loss of my idealized image of a father. With this realization, I moved beyond forgiveness and into compassion. I didn't exactly forgive him; instead, I forgave myself for never truly seeing him. Until that moment, I couldn't mourn the loss of the father I wished I had.

This process doesn't excuse others' behaviors, but it helps us acknowledge our expectations and prevent them from harming our relationships. Mourning these "little deaths" with compassion instead of judgment frees us from the weight of unmet expectations.

By confronting these shadows with love and understanding, we learn to navigate life not with resentment but with a heart ready to forgive and embrace whatever comes next, freeing ourselves to truly live. In this act of truly living, we prepare ourselves to face death with peace and acceptance.

MEDITATIVE QUESTIONS

Self-Responsibility and Reactions

Reflect on a recent interaction where you felt hurt or disappointed. How might shifting your perspective from "You made me feel this way" to "I feel this way when I interact with you" change the dynamic?

Unspoken Expectations

Identify any unspoken expectations you have in your relationships (romantic, familial, friendships). How have these expectations impacted your satisfaction and connection?

Spinning and Resolution

Reflect on a recurring story or conflict you find yourself "spinning." What underlying unmet expectations might be fueling this cycle?

Forgiveness and Compassion

Reflect on a person you have struggled to forgive. What unmet expectations or judgments are you holding on to?

CHAPTER 30

Coming Home to Ourselves

SINCE MY MOTHER'S passing when I was eighteen, the concept of "home" has been difficult to grasp. Although I've lived in many places and loved many of them, none have truly felt like home. People often ask me where home is, and I find it hard to answer. Over the years, the idea of home has shifted from being a physical place to an emotional state—a deep sense that everything will be okay, a feeling that disappeared the day my mother died.

This changed after a few pivotal experiences, including the profound DMT experience I detailed in a previous chapter. During this experience, I felt an overwhelming sense of perfection in existence. It allowed me to see beyond the physical world and understand a state where everything was perfect, and all my fears and anxieties vanished. This feeling didn't come from my surroundings but from within me when I was at peace. This moment of pure unencumbered bliss felt like being in the womb—complete and utter peace.

Years of chasing experiences taught me that happiness is not a destination but part of a practice. I found happiness more attainable in certain environments—whether working out, spending time in nature, engaging in passionate work, or being in a loving relationship. Setting conditions conducive to happiness made its emergence more likely.

Similarly, the concept of home for me has evolved to resemble this approach to happiness. By removing distractions and adding elements that foster peace, the feeling of being at home emerges naturally. It is in this state that I paradoxically feel closest to death—comfortable and complete, without the restless need for future assurances or past repairs.

The phrase by Ram Dass, "We are all just walking each other home," resonates deeply with me. It captures the dual sense of home I've discovered: the present peace within and the ultimate return to the essence from which we came.

A few years ago, while helping a friend with a project in Orgiva, Spain, I felt an immediate sense of home. The town's Bohemian life-style and proximity to nature immediately evoked a feeling of home, a rawness absent in the technologically saturated environments I was used to. The simple, unspoiled life of the village, free from modern distractions, mirrored the inner peace I had long sought. Here, amid the natural rhythms, life and death didn't seem like distinct or distant events but part of a continuous flow.

Though initially hesitant, Rani eventually saw the profound impact this place had on me. After many conversations and visits, we decided to buy a property there. Now, I sit on our terrace, sur-rounded by mountains, feeling more at home than I have since my mother's passing.

One evening, as the sun began to set, casting a golden tint over the landscape, Rani joined me on the roof terrace. She looked around, taking in the serene beauty of the mountains and the gentle rustling of the trees. "It's truly beautiful here," she said softly, her voice filled with a newfound appreciation.

I nodded, my eyes fixed on the horizon. "It really is. There's something about this place that just feels right."

Rani turned to me, curiosity in her eyes. "What is it about this place that makes you feel so connected?" she asked.

"It's everything," I replied, searching for the right words. "Here, in this setting, I feel connected—to the moment, to nature, to the people around me. There's a gentle surrender to life's flow, an acceptance that everything is as it should be. It's a feeling I haven't had in a long time."

She leaned back in her chair, contemplating my words. "I can see that. You've been more at peace here than anywhere else we've lived." I smiled, appreciating her understanding. "Why did you choose this location specifically?" she asked after a moment of silence.

I took a deep breath, feeling the weight of my answer. "Because this is a place where I feel at peace dying," I said quietly.

Rani's eyes widened slightly, but she didn't look shocked. Instead, she seemed to understand the depth of what I was saying. "That's a powerful statement," she said softly.

I nodded. "It is. But it's true. For the first time since my mother passed, I feel like I've found a place where I can truly be at peace with everything, including the end of life."

She reached out and took my hand, her touch warm and reassuring. "I'm glad you found this place. I'm glad we found it together."

We sat in silence for a while, watching the sun dip below the mountains. At that moment, everything felt perfectly aligned. The past, with all its pain and loss, the present, with its moments of peace and connection, and the future, with its inevitable uncertainties. Here, on this terrace, surrounded by the beauty of nature and the love of those around me, I felt a sense of home I had long thought lost.

In the stillness of that evening, I realized that finding home was not about a specific location but about creating a space where my soul could rest. It was about building an environment that nurtured my inner peace and allowed me to connect deeply with myself and others. As Rani and I watched the last light fade from the sky, I knew that we had found something truly special. This place, this moment, the home we had finally found within ourselves.

MEDITATIVE QUESTIONS

Inner Peace

Think about a moment when you felt complete peace. What conditions or factors contributed to this feeling?

Facing Mortality

Consider your feelings about mortality. How does finding a sense of home within yourself impact your perspective on death?

Creating Home

Think about the people and places that make you feel most at home. How do they contribute to your sense of belonging and peace?

Letting Go of the Past

Reflect on any experiences that have shaped your current understanding of home. How can you let go of past pains to find peace in the present?

CHAPTER 31

Guiding Our Lives with Love

THE MOST PROFOUND guide on my journey toward understanding death has been love. When reflecting on my life and preparation for the end, I often ask myself whether my actions and reactions are motivated by love or something less heartfelt. This question serves as a compass, guiding me through the darkness with a sense of direction and purpose.

Without love, my actions seem to lack meaning, feeling arbitrary at best. Sure, one decision could lead to greater wealth, another to increased prestige, but ultimately, I return to the fundamental question, "Why pursue this at all?" If love isn't part of the equation, then the pursuit feels hollow, leaving an unfillable void regardless of the wealth or accolades I might acquire.

One morning, I was with my very old friend Mina, who came to visit me in Spain. She joined me for my morning ritual of watching the sunrise over the Alpujarra mountains. Just as the sun peeked over the horizon, she turned to me with curiosity in her eyes.

"You often talk about preparing for the end. How can you actually help someone with that?" she asked.

I took a deep breath, considering her question. "It's funny because I can never say what works for others, only what's worked for me," I began. "Every day, I ask myself whether my actions and reactions are motivated by love."

Mina nodded. "That makes sense. But how does that work in practice?"

"There is a feeling that I have," I explained. "It's deep, and it's as if there are tears ready to flow at any moment. If I am getting closer to tears, then I know that I am moving closer to love."

She smiled. "So, it's about finding meaning through love?"

"Yes, in a way," I said. "Love is my north star."

She sighed, a mix of understanding and concern. "I get it, but knowing you for as long as I have, it sometimes feels like you're giving too much of yourself."

"I understand," I replied. "But love is what gives my life purpose. Without it, everything else feels empty."

On any given day, I feel like I face twenty moments to choose between love and fear. Do I open myself to love and let it steer my actions, or do I let fear drive me to withdraw? Do I smile at someone on the street or live in fear that they might misinterpret me? Do I tell someone how happy I feel to be with them, or do I hold back for fear that they might react negatively? Do I offer to help a neighbor with their groceries, or do I avoid it because I'm afraid of intruding? Do I take time to play with a child in the park, or do I stay distant because I'm worried about what others might think? Do I take a moment to compliment a stranger's outfit, or do I keep silent out of fear of being misunderstood? Every small decision is an opportunity to choose love over fear.

That evening, Mina came back to discussing the nature of love. "I heard this story about 'fish love' from Rabbi Twerski," she said, looking thoughtful. "It's about a man who claims to love fish, but really, he loves the taste and satisfaction it brings him."

I smiled, recognizing the story. "Yes, exactly. He doesn't love the fish itself; he loves what the fish gives him. It's a metaphor for how people sometimes claim to love others, but really, they love the way those people make them feel."

Mina nodded. "So, it's about selfishness versus selflessness?"

"Yes," I replied. "I have always felt love is about giving without expecting anything in return. It's about caring for someone else's well-being, not just what they can do for you."

Understanding the difference between fish love and this deeper love has profound implications for how we approach our relationships. Fish love, with its focus on personal gain, often leaves us feeling empty and unfulfilled. In contrast, this deeper love, rooted in selflessness, has the potential to bring richer connection and fulfillment.

This broader understanding of love has been crucial as I think about my own mortality. Feeling connected to love gives my life meaning and helps me see death as a natural part of life. I've realized that love isn't just about people; it also connects me to animals, plants, and even objects. This connection creates a comforting sense of existence.

As I approach the later years of my life, my conversations have shifted from accomplishments to acts of kindness and service. I see the presence of love in my life as a series of flowers left behind, each one representing an act of kindness that continues to spread through others. It's a force that moves through the world, growing and evolving.

Living guided by love means not letting fear steer me. It means following my heart, even when it's challenging. This approach has not only prepared me for my eventual passing but has enriched every moment up to it, making my life a continuous expression of love.

MEDITATIVE QUESTIONS

Daily Choices

Consider a typical day. How often do you face moments where you can choose between love and fear? Can you identify specific instances?

Acts of Kindness

Think about recent acts of kindness you've performed. How did these actions make you feel, both in the moment and afterward?

Approaching Mortality

Consider how the presence of love in your life influences your perception of mortality. Does it bring you comfort and acceptance?

Living with Love

Think about a challenging situation you are currently facing. How can approaching it with love instead of fear change the outcome or your experience of it?

CHAPTER 32

My Death Wish

I'VE ALWAYS FOUND breathing deeply challenging. It's as if drawing breath high into my lungs is a form of self-protection, similar to a wary cat unwilling to expose its belly until it feels completely safe. This shallow breathing was never a problem per se, just a peculiarity I noticed about myself. It made me wonder, *what would life be like if I could relax more deeply into my breath?*

To explore this, I embarked on a holotropic breathwork course. Holotropic breathwork can be described as an approach to achieve a state not all that dissimilar to a psychedelic experience, but without drugs. Imagine being in a serene, spacious room, devoid of mental clutter, or floating in perfectly temperate water. This practice can lead to profound, sometimes life-altering insights.

During one session, the instructor guided us through the process.

"Begin by finding a comfortable position," she said, her voice calm and soothing. "Close your eyes, relax your jaw, and start to take deep, controlled breaths. Let the music guide you."

I followed her instructions, allowing my breaths to deepen into my belly. The rhythmic music filled the room, creating a tranquil atmosphere.

"Keep breathing deeply," she continued. "As you inhale, imagine drawing in not just air, but also the energy of life itself. Let go of any tension in your body and mind. Allow yourself to be fully present in this moment, trusting that your breath can take you to places deep within your consciousness."

As I maintained the controlled rhythm, a wave of euphoria enveloped me. It felt like a transcendental state—intense, yet different from my experiences with DMT. Instead of flying through the cosmos, I was settling deeply into my body. The most striking similarity was the silencing of the white noise in my brain. In an instant, I found myself lying on my imaginary deathbed.

"Feel the breath opening pathways within you," the instructor's voice continued, "illuminating hidden corners of your mind and soul. Each breath is a step deeper into your inner landscape, where profound insights and connections await."

I was having a vision of my final moments. It was a serene departure, surrounded by everyone I've ever loved. Some touched my hand, tears mingling with smiles; others grappled with their emotions. Though I couldn't speak, I felt a profound connection, as if communicating on the deepest of levels. I was back in the experience of everything feeling connected on a cosmic level.

In this vision, the boundaries of spoken words dissolved, replaced by an unspoken understanding that transcended language. It was reminiscent of how I communicated with a friend as she was dying of cancer. The love and presence of those around me created a palpable sense of peace and completion. This serene image reaffirmed my belief in the power of love to transcend even the final moments of life, transforming them from an end into a continuation of the connections we've cultivated throughout our lives.

"I love you. I always have. Don't be sad—it's okay," I conveyed silently, my thoughts wrapping around them like a warm embrace. "Thank you for being here. Let this be a time of joy, a reminder to focus on what truly matters in the life you still have. Cherish these moments and hold on to the beauty of now."

Surprisingly, in this vision, no one was absent—not even those

I'd been estranged from. Their presence was as comforting as that of lifelong friends. It was a revelation to feel such universal love and acceptance, recognizing that, in this imagined final moment, everyone was perfect, just as they were.

Most of us don't get to choose our end, be it sudden like an accident, or slow like illness. Either way, I have to imagine it brings a shock, a profound disorientation unlike anything else. My own brush with this came when a car I was in skidded off a mountain road as a teenager. Time dilated, each second stretched out, and the world slowed down as we tumbled. Time seemed to take on an infinite quality.

The car flipped multiple times, yet during those moments, there was an eerie, prolonged calm. That instant mirrored what I imagine the shock of death might be like—a sudden plunge into a moment that stretches our perception of time and reality. It's a state I've come to appreciate, even finding a sense of beauty and magic in it. I often wonder if this is what the end feels like.

Cees, my mentor, once shared his curiosity about the dying process, looking forward to experiencing it despite the obvious end it signified. "I'm curious how it will feel," he mused, "to have each motor function shut down, to slowly drift back to our origins." His subsequent death while visiting his first silent retreat only deepened my reflection on his words.

His perspective shifted my own. While the thought of death is disturbing, the process itself—this final act of letting go—can be a profound experience. It's a passage we all must take alone, yet it intimately connects us to the cycle of life and death.

Today, my work continues Cees' legacy, shaping the content of the books I write, including this one. Through these pages, I hope to inspire others as he inspired me, fostering actions that ripple forward, impacting lives beyond our own.

My wish for both my death and life is to embrace each moment as precious, seeing the end not with fear but as a natural, celebrated transition—a final act of love and a testament to a life lived fully and deeply.

MEDITATIVE QUESTIONS

Embracing Breath and Life

Reflect on your own breathing patterns. How often do you notice yourself breathing shallowly? What circumstances or feel ngs might contribute to this habit?

Visualizing the End

Imagine your own final moments. Who would you want to be present, and what would you want to communicate to them?

Curiosity and the Dying Process

Reflect on Cees' curiosity about the dying process. How do you feel about the idea of experiencing death as a final act of letting go?

Final Wishes

What are your wishes for your own death? How can you start living in a way that aligns with those wishes?

CHAPTER 33

My Last Day

WHEN RANI ASKS about my day, I usually take a moment to think before I answer. On tough days, I might say something like, "Today didn't feel like I was ready to die." This feeling, filled with a sense of missing something vital, underscores how deeply I value being fully present in every moment.

Feeling ready for death is a significant part of my daily life. Days filled with frustration, stress, or fear feel like "lost days" to me. If it all ended today, I'd scratch my head and think, "Really? That's how I spent my last day?" Since I never really know when my last day will be, I try to appreciate each moment and let this awareness guide my choices. I pay attention to environments that disrupt my peace of mind and try to avoid them as much as possible. At the same time, I recognize that it's not just physical locations that can pull me away.

For instance, a friend who sees untapped potential in my work often urges me to monetize my content.

"This content is gold. We can turn this into a great business," he insists, proposing strategies to build a marketing funnel.

"How do you figure?" I asked, curious but cautious.

"Well, imagine this," he started enthusiastically, "we offer free valuable content to attract followers, build an email list, and then escalate offers with premium content. Step-by-step, we create a stream of revenue."

As he outlined the steps, a sinking sensation overcame me. Instead of feeling excited, I felt a familiar internal conflict—a clash between the thrill of a business opportunity and my yearning for peace of mind. The thought of being consumed by the demands of success while sacrificing my authentic self was discomforting.

"But won't that change my free time?" I asked, trying to reconcile his vision with my own.

"It will enhance it," he replied, "giving you a broader reach with less effort."

I nodded slowly, still feeling the weight of the decision. "I appreciate the potential, but I worry about losing the essence of why I started this in the first place."

He leaned back, understanding dawning in his eyes. "I get it. It's a lot to consider. Just don't forget the value you already bring to so many."

I smiled, grateful for his perspective, even as I continued to wrestle with finding a balance between my passion and the patience needed to move at a comfortable pace.

In these moments, I confront a critical question: am I shying away from a challenge, or am I truly honoring my well-being? Reflecting on this helps me distinguish between genuine aspirations and ego-driven pursuits. When proposals don't elicit a resounding internal "Hell yes," I question their value and purpose in my life. Such undertakings often demand a substantial investment of time and energy without leading me where I really desire - deeper fulfillment. The question I ask myself is, "Why am I really doing this?"

Prioritizing is really important here. For some people, inner peace and calm might not be a big deal, and that's totally fine. But for me, they are essential. Without inner peace, I lose touch with who I am, which affects how much I can support those I work with. They come to me not just for my advice, but also for the sense of peace they feel around me. This peace comes from dealing with my own issues, including my fears around death.

Of course, peace and calm were nowhere in sight for the first forty-plus years of my life. For decades, I needed help but didn't know how to ask for it. After my mother died, I shut down emotionally, making it difficult for anyone to reach me. There was one exception—Jane. Receiving love after experiencing the pain of its loss is incredibly vulnerable. Jane saw me, not by trying to fix me, but by treating me like her son. Writing about this is challenging because being loved that deeply by another person can be overwhelming. It's this feeling that I hope to impart to others in my interactions with them.

It was not that long after Jane had given me that sense of family that she was diagnosed with terminal cancer. I was living in Japan at the time, but I made a few trips back to see her.

On my last visit, she was in a very bad state—gray and frail. Each moment felt like it could be the last. She was in a room with a window looking out to the backyard. I used some money from the school I worked at in Japan to buy her a gift. I went to the garden center and planted a small field of flowers for her to look at from the window. It was something beautiful for her to enjoy as she let go of her body.

I spent a lot of time at her bedside, which was not easy. The house was filled with emotional pain, and her family struggled to be with her in her suffering. They too were suffering, and there was no one to counsel and support everyone through the process. I sat next to her bed, feeling deeply helpless.

As we sat together, she would groan and drift in and out of consciousness. When she awoke, she would hold my hand and look deeply into my eyes. I don't believe I have ever communicated so deeply with someone without speaking. We simply observed and sat with a profound understanding.

One moment that will stay with me forever occurred when I was holding her hand for most of the day, alone. Although the family was in the house, it was emotionally painful for them to be in the room. Her youngest son would walk in and out of his room, which was visible from the bed down the hallway. We saw him walk in with his head down, avoiding any contact. We looked at each other, acknowledging the pain he was going through. It shocked me that she was observing his pain while enduring her own. Years later, I learned how sensitive I am to others' pain when I am raw to my own.

As she looked at me, she said, "When the time comes, let him know." Her words were overwhelming. I knew exactly what she meant, even though she said so little. It is in these intense moments of living that we feel the deepest connections. It was my first experience being with someone on their last day, and it helped me understand the intensity of emotion that is hard to imagine in the everyday noise that drowns it out.

Twenty years later, I called her son and shared that moment with him. She and I both knew he would hold regret for not being able to sit with his pain as he watched his mother deteriorate in front of his eyes. When I shared the moment with him, he broke down in tears. He realized that his mother understood and was neither resentful nor disappointed. She simply saw the helplessness in everyone. It's in these moments that we truly have the opportunity to see one another.

Now, as Rani and I face a temporary separation due to a business trip, our parting always carries a sadness.

"Andy, I can't believe you're going away again," Rani said, her voice heavy with emotion. "It always feels so painful."

"I know," I replied softly. "I'm reminded that one day there will be a last time we say goodbye."

Rani looked at me with tears in her eyes. "I know. It sucks."

"I have to say that I'm grateful we get to feel this way," I shared.

"Really? How does that work?" she asked.

"Imagine if we didn't feel this way, if it was easy to go away. That would suck more. The pain reminds me just how much I love you," I said.

"Well, I like your perspective, but it still sucks," Rani concluded.

Over time, I've learned to see these moments of sadness as opportunities to deepen our bond. The intense emotion underscores how deeply I care, transforming sadness into a profound connection.

Through the journey of losing loved ones and facing my own vulnerabilities, I've learned to trust in love again. I recognize the risks, but I embrace the depth it brings to my life. Living each day as if it might be my last has made my life richer. This mindset has transformed my life from just existing to truly engaging with the world in a meaningful way.

MEDITATIVE QUESTIONS

Love and Connection

Think about a person who has had a profound impact on your life, like Jane did for me. How can you honor their memory and influence in your daily life?

Transforming Sadness into Connection

How can you transform moments of sadness into opportunities to deepen your bond with others? What role does vulnerability play in this process?

Living with Intention

How can you integrate the practice of living each day as if it were your last into your daily routine? What changes might this bring about?

CLOSING

Tomorrow, and tomorrow, and tomorrow,

Creeps in this petty pace from day to day,

To the last syllable of recorded time;

And all our yesterdays have lighted fools

The way to dusty death. Out, out, brief candle!

Life's but a walking shadow, a poor player,

That struts and frets his hour upon the stage,

And then is heard no more. It is a tale

Told by an idiot, full of sound and fury,

Signifying nothing.

THESE HAUNTING LINES from Shakespeare's Macbeth have echoed in my mind ever since I was tasked with memorizing them in high school. I marveled at Macbeth's stark resignation, concluding his soliloquy with the grim view that life is "full of sound and fury, signifying nothing." Over the years, I've grappled with his nihilism, striving to find where Shakespeare might have erred. Indeed, we did not choose our entry into this world, but that does not strip us of the choice in how we experience our time here.

If you've come this far with me in the book, it means that we've shared moments together—this connection is what I cherish most in life and why I am driven to write. Our perspectives might differ, shaped by distinct experiences, yet beneath it all, there exists a universal thread of humanity that binds us.

Through this exploration of death, my aim has been for you to gain insights into your life, to understand what matters most to you, and to embrace love—not just the love between us but a love that encompasses all beings and things.

As I delve deeper into my own mortality, I've come closer to truly living. You and I are now kindred spirits, bound by this text. I hold love for you and cherish the hope that we might one day meet, look each other in the eyes, and share a laugh—acknowledging together the absurd beauty of life